# MASTERING CLASSIC COCKTAILS

## Recipes and Techniques for the Home Bartender

**C. Townsend Brady**

Design by Diana Russell Piazza

Photography by Rod Searcey

ISBN: 978-1-9839398-9-4 (hardcover)


Photography: Rod Searcey, RodSearcey.com

Design: Diana Russell Piazza, DianaRussellDesign.com

Copyeditor: Mark Woodworth, Editmarks@weebly.com

Publishing Strategist: Holly Brady, HollyBrady.com


Please direct comments or permission requests to:
bradyct@gmail.com


Palo Alto Publishing
Palo Alto, CA 94306

This book is dedicated to all the professional
bartenders who—as I sat at their bars during a quiet period—
patiently listened to my questions and offered multiple
suggestions as to how I could become better at their craft.
They taught me so much.

# CONTENTS

# ACKNOWLEDGMENTS

A GREAT MANY people encouraged me and helped me with this project.

First on the list is my talented wife, Holly. We both graduated with English degrees from Stanford University many decades ago, but Holly clearly outranks me when it comes to postgraduate writing skills. Over the years, and not without substantial effort, she has made me a better writer. And her career in book publishing has helped me enormously in shaping this book.

My good friend Rod Searcey, a talented professional photographer, is responsible for all the stunning photos herein.

Diana Russell Piazza created the elegant book design and layout. She has brought to bear on this project her years as designer for Meredith Books and Better Homes and Gardens cookbooks, and it shows.

My daughter, Cait, and her husband, David Gaber, enthusiastically supported the project by introducing me to many different whiskeys and aperitifs, and by enduring countless cocktail tastings.

My brother Terry and his wife, Lisa, pointed me in the direction of many high-end cocktail ingredients and made key suggestions as to how to improve certain cocktails.

Nancy and Ed Bradley, two Martini epicures, were instrumental in helping me fine-tune my Martini recipe. They also supported my research and education in the art of crafting fine cocktails. I am most grateful to them for their ongoing encouragement.

Finally, I want to thank the many colleagues and friends who were so appreciative of the various classic cocktails I served them over the years. Their encouragement kept me motivated. These include Gina Anderson; Sandy Baron; Susan Brady; Alison Bradywood; Gayle Brugler; Robin Ellis; Farrokh Farrokhi; Chuck and Polly Gaber; Kerry Givens; Lynn Glover; Karen Guttieri; Frank Guzzone; Contessa Hannig; Tib Hotson; Roland Hsu; Annie Kolar; Ellie Laney; Rosemarie Menager; Mary and Barb Martin; Avy Nielsen; Julie Noblitt; Judy Ocken; Judy Ocken; Bill, Helen, and Dan Pflaum; John Piazza; Mark Rhysburger; Ollivette and Gary Smith; Christian Sorensen; Karen Walker; Amy, Jenny, and Meredith Wheeler; Jackie Wheeler; Mark Woodworth; and Gary and Susan Zweig.

# INTRODUCTION

IN HIS 1948 classic *The Fine Art of Mixing Drinks,* David Embury made the claim that anyone can make a good cocktail—but few people actually do. And he included many professional bartenders in this criticism.

Embury's book quickly became a classic in the cocktail industry. Some cocktail bars even made it required reading for their new bartenders. A lawyer by profession, Embury commented that his book was written *by* an amateur *for* amateurs. But when you read his book, you will quickly conclude he was an extremely knowledgeable home bartender.

In the interest of full disclosure, the book you are now holding is written by another home bartender and is intended for home bartenders who are interested in becoming skilled at the art of mixing classic cocktails.

I agree with David Embury that anyone can make a good cocktail. If you dedicate yourself to mastering the recipes and techniques in this book, you will soon be making cocktails that rival and even surpass those made at your favorite local bar or most bars you encounter in your travels. Here's why:

- Unlike a professional bartender, you are not constrained by the need to make a profit, so you can afford to use higher quality spirits. Such spirits generally contribute to better-tasting cocktails.

- You can select specific brands of base spirits (whiskey, gin, vodka, rum, tequila); combine them with liqueurs, syrups, or fortified wines; and then fine-tune the ratio of ingredients so that the cocktail becomes perfect *for you.*

- You can use techniques that are not employed in most commercial bars. Cutting the peel of citrus fruit with a channel knife so that a micro-spray of zest oil sprays directly onto the surface of a cocktail is one example. This technique alone elevates many cocktails from good to great. "Superchilling" a cocktail, such as a Martini, to get it cold enough for your personal preference without overdiluting it is another. Both of those techniques are covered in Chapter 2: Guidelines for Great Cocktails.

- You can use the highest quality citrus fruits and squeeze them fresh for each cocktail. Some commercial bars follow this protocol, but not all.

Which cocktails are included here? William Grimes, restaurant critic for the *New York Times*, points out in his cocktail book *Straight Up or On the Rocks* that most cocktails, like most paintings or plays, are *bad*. Grimes might have been a bit harsh in his criticism. I think *mediocre* might be a better term. But whatever the term, most cocktails are simply not worth drinking. Consequently, the scope of this book is limited to a highly select group of *classic* cocktails, most of which are 65 to well over 100 years old. It is further limited to those classic cocktails that I consider to be the best of the best. I know some people might be disappointed that the Aviation, the Last Word, and other classics didn't make the final cut for this book. My apologies if your favorite classic cocktail is not included.

This book is different from many cocktail books, in that it goes well beyond merely listing recipe ingredients. In both the introductory chapters and the individual recipes, I have emphasized techniques for constructing cocktails. I own over 40 cocktail books, and the ones that taught me the most were those that emphasized technique.

I also recommend specific brands of base spirits, liqueurs, and fortified wines in my recipes. I find that a specific brand can make a substantial difference between an ordinary cocktail and a memorable one. Obviously, this is a subjective judgment on my part, and you may not agree with every recommendation.

In addition, I include the history of each cocktail. Knowing a cocktail's history and relating it to your guests will make each cocktail just a little more special.

Finally, I identify the cocktails that have become my personal favorites.

I hope this book will enable you to become proficient at constructing some of the finest classic cocktails. In the process, my guess is that, in addition to drinking well, you will reap a few other benefits:

- When you sit at a good bar and drink a cocktail, you will find yourself one of the more-knowledgeable patrons at that bar. And if the bar is not crowded, you'll find that most bartenders like to interact with customers who understand and appreciate the nuances of their craft.

- You may well become a popular host. People *love* hosts who can make fine cocktails, particularly when you introduce them to a classic they've never tried before.

- You will enjoy the absolute pleasure that comes with mastering any skill.

As one of my friends commented, learning to make classic cocktails well is a sophisticated activity. It's also an extremely enjoyable one. I hope you find as much pleasure in it as I have.

Cheers,

C.T.B.

Palo Alto, California

# CHAPTER 1

# A BRIEF HISTORY OF COCKTAILS

THERE ARE TWO misconceptions concerning the history of cocktails. One is that the United States was their birthplace. The other is that the Prohibition era of the 1920s was a major factor in the development of new cocktails.

In fact, cocktails were decidedly *not* a United States invention. One theory claims they evolved in the Caribbean in the sixteenth century. It is said that in 1586 the sailors on a fleet of ships under the command of Sir Francis Drake, while pillaging Spanish ports in the Caribbean, began to suffer from serious cases of scurvy. Drake's cousin Richard Drake went ashore and met with native Indians who consumed a beverage made with a rum-like spirit called *aguardiente,* which was mixed with lime juice, sugarcane juice, and mint. Richard brought back quantities of the drink, which the sailors consumed, and the lime juice in their drinks cured the crew's scurvy.

The Spanish who had settled the Caribbean continued to enjoy this cocktail, naming it *El Draque*—the nickname they gave to Sir Francis Drake, which also means "the Devil." Based on its ingredients, *El Draque* was clearly a close cousin to the Mojito. It had been around for at least two decades before our nation's first colonists arrived at Jamestown.

A second theory concerning the evolution of cocktails proposes they evolved in England from punch. The word *punch* is derived from a Hindi word meaning *five.* Early Indian punch recipes were usually prepared with five ingredients—citrus juice, sugar, water, spices, and alcohol. In the mid-1600s, sailors returning from India brought back recipes for punch to their home country, and punch bars soon became commonplace in London.

According to cocktail historian David Wondrich, James Ashley opened the London Coffee and Punch House in 1731, where he offered traditional large bowls of punch. But he also began to innovate by mixing single servings of the drink. These single-serving preparations would clearly qualify as "cocktails" in today's terminology.

But America *did* play a significant role in the subsequent growth of the cocktail. Since the purity of local water in the colonies was sometimes questionable, colonists often preferred drinks containing alcohol—a safer alternative. That might explain why colonists reputedly consumed alcohol at twice the level we do today. While beer was the staple offering, tavern owners soon began to experiment with new ways to serve stronger spirits.

Soon colonists began to distill their own spirits. In her book *Drinking in America,* Susan Cheever notes that even before the American Revolution an astounding 159 rum distilleries had arisen in New England. These distilleries imported huge quantities of molasses from the Caribbean to produce their rum.

If colonial New England was known for its rum production, New Jersey became famous for its apple brandy. Initially, apple cider was fermented into hard cider, and then it was distilled through a technique known as freeze-distillation. A farmer would place a barrel of hard cider out on his porch for the winter. When the temperature

*Sir Francis Drake*

dropped below 32°F, the water in the hard cider would freeze, producing a sheet of ice floating on top of the cider. By simply removing the sheet of ice, the farmer achieved a higher alcohol content in the remaining cider. By the end of winter, the hard cider would evolve into a full-bodied apple brandy, which the colonists named applejack. Freeze-distillation was adequate for a family farmer, but distilleries were needed for quantity production. By the 1830s some 388 distilleries were producing applejack in New Jersey alone. As a result, applejack acquired the nickname *Jersey Lightning*.

Colonial Pennsylvanians produced rye whiskey because rye grew well in that region. After the American Revolution, Alexander Hamilton imposed a tax on whiskey to pay for war debts. Some Pennsylvania rye distillers, believing the tax extremely unfair, responded by literally tarring and feathering tax collectors in what is known as the Whiskey Rebellion. George Washington dispatched an army of 13,000 soldiers to end that rebellion.

*The Whiskey Rebellion*

As colonists moved west, they discovered that the region that would later become Kentucky and Tennessee was more suited to growing corn than rye, so that area became known for corn whiskey. Corn whiskey that met a specific set of high standards took on the name Bourbon.

Bourbon, rye, applejack, and rum all ended up in early American taverns. Since distillers likely needed to make a quick return on their labor, aged spirits were probably a rarity. One motivation for early American bartenders to create cocktails might simply have been to mellow out the rough young spirits of the time.

The first reference to a cocktail appeared in print, without definition, in an 1803 edition of a New Hampshire newspaper called *The Farmer's Cabinet.* Three years later a Hudson, New York, newspaper, *The Balance and Columbian Repository,* did attempt a definition:

> A cock-tail [*sic*], then, is a stimulating liquor, composed of spirits of any kind, sugar, water, and bitters. It is vulgarly called a bittered sling, and is supposed to be an excellent electioneering potion, inasmuch as it renders the heart stout and bold, at the same time that it fuddles the head. It is said also to be of great use to a democratic candidate: because, a person having swallowed a glass of it is ready to swallow anything else.

The cocktail described above would come to be known as the Old Fashioned.

When it comes to the derivation of the word *cocktail,* things get even more obscure. New Orleanians claim that the nation's first cocktail was created by a French-speaking Haitian immigrant—Antoine Peychaud (1803–1883)—who served it in an egg cup known as a *coquetier.* That word, they say, was later anglicized as *cocktail.* But this claim doesn't hold much water, since the word *cocktail* was first published in *The Balance and Columbian Repository* in 1806 when Peychaud was just three years old.

Other stories about the derivation of the word *cocktail* are often floated, but David Wondrich has certainly come up with the most colorful one. Wondrich writes that in colonial times, if you wanted to sell an older horse, you wanted it to look young and frisky. One of the attributes of a young horse is that it holds its tail high. A seller of an older horse would sometimes stick a piece of ginger up the horse's butt to make it cock up its tail.

Early Americans had few inhibitions about drinking before noon. Legend has it that some Southern plantation owners began their morning with a Mint Julep and kept imbibing throughout the day.

In the early 1800s, Frederick Tudor achieved a major breakthrough for cocktails when he started harvesting ice from Massachusetts ponds in the winter. Tudor found that if he packed the ice in sawdust, it would remain cold during both storage and shipment, enabling him to ship ice halfway around the world. Thanks to Tudor, chilled cocktails became possible in any season, anywhere in our country.

The period from the 1860s to Prohibition is known as the Golden Age of Cocktails. Classic cocktails such as the Martini and Manhattan were conceived during this period. At the same time, anxiety grew over the nation's level of alcohol consumption. Temperance movements proliferated and eventually won the day. On January 16, 1919, the Eighteenth Amendment to the Constitution was ratified, outlawing the manufacture, sale, or transport of alcoholic beverages meant for public consumption. One year later, the Volstead Act enforced that amendment, and Prohibition began. It was nicknamed *The Noble Experiment*, but, as we will see, it produced some ignoble consequences.

Some claim that cocktails flourished during Prohibition as bartenders struggled to improve the flavor of low-quality spirits by adding more-palatable ingredients. While a few cocktails, such as the Bee's Knees, did get created this way, Prohibition was essentially the nadir for cocktail culture in America. High-quality spirits were hard to come by, and some of the country's best bartenders migrated for their livelihood to Cuba or Europe.

Prohibition reduced the supply of liquor, but it had little effect on the nation's demand for it. Organized crime addressed this demand by both bootlegging and reprocessing denatured industrial alcohol. The government had little success in stopping bootlegging, but they began to curb the reprocessing of industrial alcohol by adding various compounds—including methyl alcohol, kerosene, and benzine—to make the resulting liquor unpalatable. Despite the government's strategy, organized crime continued their reprocessing efforts, producing liquor that often contained unsafe levels of toxins. By some estimates as many as 10,000 people died from drinking toxic liquor. Senator Edward I. Edwards of New Jersey condemned the government's strategy at the time as "legalized murder."

*Spirits poured into sewer during Prohibition*

The Noble Experiment clearly did not work as expected, and on December 5, 1933, Prohibition was ended by the ratification of the Twenty-First Amendment. One of the few good outcomes of Prohibition was that women, who had been excluded from most pre-Prohibition saloons, were warmly received in Prohibition speakeasies and continued to be accepted in the now-legal bars.

With the advent of World War II, the cocktail industry took another hit. Government mandates directed distilleries to stop producing beverage alcohol, and instead to make industrial-grade alcohol for various uses in the war effort.

After the war ended and American life returned to normal, a wave of processed foods came onto the market. Bottled and frozen cocktail mixers appeared in both commercial and home bars. As convenience took precedence over taste, almost anyone could be a bartender. All one had to do was add an alcoholic spirit to these mixers, chill, and serve. Legend has it that during this period President Kennedy and his wife, Jackie, regularly enjoyed Daiquiris at the end of the workday. In spite of the fact that they had extensive kitchen staff at their beck and call, their Daiquiris were made with frozen concentrated limeade. A third difficult period for cocktails in this nation had begun.

At the same time, vodka was rising in popularity. Because vodka lacks the strong flavors of whiskey or gin, it's easier for novice drinkers to enjoy. By 1970 it was the best-selling spirit in the country, with cocktails made from vodka eclipsing such classics as the Gin Martini and Manhattan.

Who rescued us from this cocktail drought? Many people credit Dale Degroff, head bartender at New York's famous Rainbow Room in the 1980s. His boss, Joseph Baum, challenged Degroff to bring back pre-Prohibition cocktail recipes and techniques to tempt and delight their patrons. Degroff responded by making his premium cocktails with freshly squeezed juices and quality spirits. But his real contribution was to share his methodology with young bartenders, including Audrey Saunders, Sasha Petraske, and Julie Reiner. Like Degroff, they became industry legends. The revolution that started in New York swept across the nation and on to Europe. Thus began the second Golden Age of Cocktails. Fortunately for all of us, it's still going strong today.

# CHAPTER 2

# GUIDELINES FOR GREAT COCKTAILS

## Guideline #1.

### Quality Cocktails Call for Decent-Quality Spirits

Use good-quality base spirits, liqueurs, and vermouths for your drinks. If you use bargain brands of liquor, your cocktails will not be as good as they could be. This rule can be particularly important in cocktails that are served "straight up" in a martini glass, such as a Martini, Manhattan, or Boulevardier. The base spirit and vermouth play a major role in these cocktails, as opposed to cocktails served in a collins or highball glass, which are often substantially diluted with tonic water or club soda.

## Guideline #2.

### Fine-Tune Classic Cocktail Recipes to Maximize Your Own Enjoyment

As part of my research to become better at mixing drinks, I purchased dozens of cocktail books written by some of today's leading bartenders and cocktail writers. When I compared how these industry leaders prepared the very same "classic cocktail," the results surprised me. Even though these are classic cocktails that have been around for roughly 100 years, most of the recipes vary slightly in ratios of base spirits, liqueurs, vermouths, or citrus juice to construct the same classic cocktail.

Part of the reason for this is that people have differing taste perceptions. Dr. Linda Bartoshuk, a psychologist working at Yale University, studied variations in people's ability to taste and discovered that people fall into three groups: *supertasters*, *medium tasters*, and *nontasters*. For supertasters, bitter foods taste even more bitter, and sweet things taste sweeter. So, a *supertaster* will probably experience a cocktail different from how it registers to a *medium taster* or a *nontaster*. Bartoshuk's study determined that *supertasters* comprise roughly 25 percent of the population, while *nontasters* comprise another 25 percent.

From my own observations, I believe that seasoned drinkers are more likely to prefer a cocktail with a stronger alcohol flavor, while less-seasoned drinkers seem to prefer drinks that are sweeter, with less alcohol flavor.

So, feel free to fine-tune a recipe to enhance your enjoyment of that cocktail. For instance, if a 3:1 ratio of gin to vermouth makes a Martini too gentle for you, consider raising the ratio to 5:1.

Note, however, that if you start adding dramatically new ingredients to a cocktail, you are no longer fine-tuning; you are creating a new drink.

## Guideline #3.
### Strive for Proper Balance in Your Cocktails

As Jason Kosmas and Dushan Zaric observe in their excellent book *Speakeasy,* achieving the correct balance among a cocktail's ingredients is paramount to making what we might consider a great cocktail. In a perfectly balanced cocktail, the ingredients work together and enhance each other. I find it helpful to focus on what I think of as three distinct aspects of cocktail balance:

- *Balance between base spirits and other ingredients*
  You want to be able to taste the base alcohol, but not be overwhelmed by it. The purpose of the other ingredients in the cocktail is to make the base spirit taste better than if it were simply served "neat." The eternal quest for the perfect Gin Martini is primarily the search for the proper balance between the gin and the vermouth. You want to be able to taste the gin, while adding just enough vermouth to smooth it out and enhance the overall flavor of the cocktail.

- ***Balance between sweet and sour***
The sweet-sour balance relates to achieving the right level of sweetness in a cocktail. Sugar syrups, fruit syrups, and some liqueurs, such as Cointreau, deliver sweetness in a drink. And lemons and limes provide the tartness. If a drink lacks the right balance of sweet and sour, the cocktail is not nearly as enjoyable as it could be. Most cocktails are best when the sweet-sour balance is just slightly on the tart side.

- ***Balance between strong-flavored liqueurs and the rest of the cocktail***
This important balance comes into play in those cocktails that use liqueurs, such as Maraschino Liqueur or Crème de Violette. These liqueurs can add a level of complexity to a cocktail, but they can also quickly overpower a drink if not used with a great deal of restraint. When that happens, all you end up tasting is the strong-flavored liqueur. For example, most recipes for Constante's Daiquiri #3 call for so much Maraschino Liqueur that its perfume-like flavor overwhelms the cocktail. My recipe for this cocktail cuts back dramatically on that ingredient, to achieve a better-balanced drink.

## Guideline #4.
### Use the Aromatic Oils from Citrus Zest to Enhance Your Cocktails

The citrus zest oil on the surface of a cocktail can often make the difference between a decent cocktail and a superb one. It is one of the great secrets in the cocktail industry. We've all encountered the wonderful aroma of citrus zest oil at one time or another. If you've ever walked into a room where someone is peeling a navel orange, you've experienced the wonderful aroma of fruit as it fills the room. But the aroma is *not* actually from the juice of the orange. Rather, it's from the orange zest oil that is released as a micro-spray when the peel is pulled from the fruit. Adding citrus zest oil is especially effective with stirred cocktails, but it can be appropriate for other cocktails, as well.

To properly utilize citrus zest oils in your cocktails, it's important to understand the anatomy of a citrus peel. The colorful outer portion of the peel is called the zest; it contains the aromatic zest oil that adds both flavor and aroma to your cocktails. Directly under that outer layer is a thicker white part called the pith. Unlike the zest, the pith can contribute to bitterness and negatively affect the taste of your cocktail. The art of using the zest is to remove the colored peel, while leaving almost all of the white pith behind. There are three basic cocktail tools that can help you in this process:

- ***Channel Knife***

  A channel knife features a sharp blade that cuts a shallow, ¼-inch-wide channel in the surface of a piece of citrus fruit. The best technique to get citrus zest oil onto the surface of a cocktail is to cut a strip of zest with this knife positioned about one inch above your cocktail. It should be positioned under the citrus fruit and just above the cocktail, so a micro-spray of zest oil goes directly onto the surface of the drink. Since the oil is lighter than the other liquids, it floats on the surface of the cocktail, creating both a nice aroma and a wonderful taste with each sip.

  Once you've finished cutting off a strip of citrus zest, twist it into a corkscrew around the handle of your barspoon and slide it off the end. You now have the proverbial "citrus twist," one end of which you can hang over the rim of a glass as a visual garnish. Let the other end drift into the cocktail, where it will add a little more flavor to the drink.

  See Chapter 8: Recommended Bar Equipment for characteristics to look for in a good channel knife.

- **Vegetable Peeler**

  You can use vegetable peelers in several ways to add citrus zest oil to a cocktail. Some bartenders shave off a wide section of peel from a piece of citrus fruit and squeeze it to express the zest oil onto the surface of a cocktail. Dale DeGroff is famous for holding a lighted match between the peel and the cocktail so the oil erupts in a burst of flame before it lands on the surface of the cocktail. Other bartenders rub the outside of the zest around the rim of a glass to coat it with oil. But candidly, I think a channel knife, used properly, does a better job of adding oil to a cocktail.

  Still, a vegetable peeler can be most helpful with cocktails such as a Whiskey Smash or Caipirinha. The standard recipe for a Whiskey Smash asks for quarters of lemon to be muddled in the bottom of the glass. This gets both the juice and zest oil into the cocktail. But with this technique you end up getting very little oil and an imprecise amount of citrus juice, plus citrus pulp and seeds floating in the finished cocktail. A vegetable peeler can solve all these problems. Simply use the peeler to shave off several sections of lemon peel, leaving most of the bitter white pith attached to the fruit. Place the peels with their yellow sides up in an old fashioned glass. Add whiskey and muddle the peels. The oil quickly infuses the whiskey with extra lemon flavor. Then you can add a precise amount of freshly squeezed, *strained* lemon juice. It takes barely any longer than muddling chunks of fruit, but you end up with a much cleaner cocktail, a precise amount of tartness, and more flavor from the oil. This technique can also be used with limes in preparing a Caipirinha.

- **Microplane Zester**

  Another method to add citrus zest oil to a cocktail is to use a Microplane zester to grate off citrus zest from a piece of fruit and marinate that zest in the base spirit of a cocktail. A Microplane zester resembles a workshop file in shape and size, and often comes with a plastic sleeve to catch the zest that's grated off the fruit. If you do not have a Microplane zester, you can use a box grater to achieve the same results. My recipes for the Margarita and the Gimlet utilize this technique to impart a little more lime flavor into the cocktails. See these recipes for a more-complete description of this technique.

*One final comment about citrus zest oil:* a little can greatly enhance a cocktail, but, like many good things, too much can quickly overpower a drink—so some restraint is in order.

## Guideline #5.
### Prechill Glasses in the Freezer

A cocktail that is not cold enough is almost not worth drinking. Prechill your glasses—both cocktail and mixing glasses—for at least 15 minutes, preferably longer, before you make your cocktails.

## Guideline #6:
### Consider a Simple Technique to Get Cocktails Colder Without Overdiluting Them

In combination with Guideline #5, I find that a fast stirring technique (80 stirs in 25 seconds) typically produces a cocktail with a temperature in the very low 20s.

Still, I find that many of my guests prefer their Martinis and Boulevardiers slightly below 20°F. One of my guests complained that not only are Martinis served at most bars too warm, but when he asks bartenders to make sure his Martini is sufficiently chilled, the resulting cocktail is often overdiluted. In Dave Arnold's wonderful book *Liquid Intelligence,* this phenomenon is dubbed the Fundamental Law of Traditional Cocktails:

> *There is no chilling without dilution.*

> *And there is no dilution without chilling.*

How do we overcome Arnold's Law and chill a cocktail to slightly below 20°F without too much dilution? The key is to use a technique other than ice to chill the cocktail—a technique available to the home bartender. I call it *superchilling.*

I discovered superchilling when I was making Martinis for several friends, one of whom was an avid Martini fan. I served him my typical Martini, whereupon he commented that it was, well, a "nice drink." Anticipating that a few of my guests might like a second round, I'd made two more Martinis using the exact same recipe and put them in the freezer to keep them chilled. After a while, my wife noticed our Martini fan had finished his drink and came into the kitchen to get him another. She took one of the drinks from the freezer and gave it to him. As soon as he took a sip, he started *raving* about it—how it was one of the *best Martinis he had ever tasted.* The only difference was that it had been chilled in the freezer for roughly 15 minutes. That simple technique lowered the temperature of the cocktail without diluting it. The concept of *superchilling* was born.

To superchill a cocktail, prepare it as you normally would, pour the finished drink into a chilled cocktail glass, and place it in the freezer section of your refrigerator for roughly 15 minutes. Once you chill the cocktail to slightly below 20°F, you may find it smoother. You might also enjoy the way it coats your tongue from the increased viscosity that comes with lower temperatures.

Important points to remember:

- When using the recipes in this book, *don't* skip the step of stirring or shaking the cocktail with ice before you put it in the freezer. Stirring or shaking not only chills the cocktail, but more importantly adds the correct amount of water from the melted ice to properly dilute the drink. Skipping this step could result in a cocktail that's too strong or that lacks smoothness.

- *Don't* leave the cocktail in the freezer too long. Reducing the temperature substantially below 20°F will mute the flavors of most cocktails.

- Superchilling works particularly well with stronger drinks, such as Martinis and Boulevardiers, but it does *not* work as well for gentler cocktails, such as Margaritas, which lose a lot of their flavor if overchilled.

- Superchilling does *not* work well for those drinks that will later incorporate egg whites, such as the Clover Club or White Lady. Low temperatures inhibit the formation of egg-white foam.

## Guideline #7.
### Maintain Quality Control: Taste and Adjust

Sometimes when you're in a good bar, you might notice the bartender take a clean short straw, insert it into a cocktail shaker containing a chilled cocktail, cap the upper end of the straw with his finger and then put the lower end in his mouth. When he removes his finger from the top of the straw, a very small portion of the drink runs onto his tongue. Sometimes this happens with such sleight of hand that it's almost unnoticeable, but the bartender is performing this little ritual because he's determining whether he needs to adjust the taste of the finished drink.

Before you serve a cocktail, taste a small sample and adjust the finished drink, if necessary, to get it right. You can either use a clean straw or simply dip a clean teaspoon into the drink.

Tasting the finished drink is particularly important for drinks containing citrus juice, which can vary dramatically in tartness from one piece of fruit to the next.

## Guideline #8.
### Strive for Consistency by Measuring Precisely

Nothing is more frustrating than fine-tuning a cocktail until it is absolutely sublime, and then making it again a week later and have it turn out to be, well, "good," but not as good as you remember. A likely explanation is that the ratios of the ingredients in the drink changed slightly from one week to the next because of imprecise measuring. The renown cocktail experts Scott Beattie, Jeffery Morgenthaler, Sasha Petraske, and Dave Arnold all emphasize the importance of measuring cocktail ingredients  carefully by using jiggers rather than free pouring. Jeff Hollinger and Rob Schwartz, in their book *The Art of the Bar,* go one step further and suggest using measuring spoons for adding smaller quantities of ingredients. For the record, I use measuring spoons for any quantity below ½ ounce. Refer to Chapter 8: Recommended Bar Equipment for specific recommendations on jiggers and measuring spoons.

Finally, it's particularly important to measure out citrus juice precisely, rather than relying on recipes that call for "the juice of one lime," a phrase that's all too common in cocktail recipes. The amount of juice can vary dramatically from one piece of fruit to the next, depending on the size of the fruit and how recently it was picked.

## Guideline #9.
### Exercise Special Care with Opened Bottles of Vermouth

An opened bottle of vermouth is like an opened bottle of wine. The newly introduced air in the bottle oxidizes the vermouth, and in roughly a week the oxidation will begin to affect the taste of your cocktails. You can employ three strategies to combat this.

First, when you open a new bottle of vermouth, consider decanting it into smaller bottles that you can fill to the top to exclude almost all air. I use empty Schweppes 10-ounce club soda or quinine water bottles for this purpose. They have twist-top plastic caps that reseal well. As you decant the vermouth into the smaller bottles, minimize the introduction of air by avoiding the creation of bubbles during the transfer. I do this by holding the smaller bottle at an angle so the vermouth flows smoothly down the side of the smaller bottle.

Second, I store all vermouths and other aperitif wines in the refrigerator after they have been opened. This also helps slow down spoilage.

Third, to any partially filled bottle I add Private Preserve, a trademarked pressurized can of inert gases that creates a blanket over the surface of the vermouth. This keeps oxygen from coming into contact with and spoiling the vermouth. Private Preserve is available from most fine liquor stores. I confess that that before I discovered it, I tried Vacu Vin, which consists of a pump with a rubber seal that is used to pump out the air from a partially filled bottle. Unfortunately, the vermouth on which I used Vacu Vin quickly began to lose its freshness. I've since come across the expression "Friends don't let Friends Vacu-Vin" (Google it!). From my experience, a can of Private Preserve is a far-superior solution.

## Guideline #10.
### Use Top-Quality Ice to Chill Your Cocktails

Approximately one-fourth of the volume of a typical cocktail served straight up is water from the ice stirred or shaken with the drink to chill it. As a result, cocktail writers place a tremendous emphasis on using top-quality ice, with solutions ranging from buying ice from a professional ice supplier to using distilled water to make ice.

I'm lucky enough to have high-quality tap water, but I still use a small PUR water filter pitcher to make my ice cubes.

If the freezer section of your refrigerator is relatively odor free, keep life simple and make your ice cubes in open ice trays. However, if the air in your freezer has any trace of odors, your ice may take on added flavors. Scott Beattie, in *Artisanal Cocktails,* suggests covering ice trays tightly with plastic wrap before placing them in the freezer, to protect them from freezer odors. But OXO has a better way: that company offers two designs of trays with tight-fitting lids that address the issue quite well.

## Guideline #11.
### Use Smaller-Capacity Martini Glasses

In an age when so many items have become supersized, martini glasses are no exception. The typical martini glass today holds somewhere between 8 and 10 ounces. That's *dramatically* larger than martini glasses from the 1930s and '40s. In *The Fine Art of Mixing Drinks,* David Embury notes that martini glasses in 1948 held some 2 to 3½ ounces.

Serving a large cocktail in a high-capacity glass means the drink becomes warm before you or your guest finishes it. It's far preferable to serve everybody two smaller cocktails in succession, rather than one large one that loses it chill before it is finished.

I recommend purchasing a set of smaller martini glasses. Riedel's Vinum Martini Glasses, each with a capacity of 4.6 ounces, are available online. These glasses, made of high-end crystal, are very elegant, though somewhat fragile.

## Guideline #12.
### Use Only Freshly Squeezed Juices from Recently Ripened Citrus

Freshly squeezed juices have a bright tartness that enhances any cocktail. I recommend using only freshly squeezed juice—not frozen, not bottled, and absolutely never canned. I look for fruit that's heavy for its size, something that indicates

a higher juice content, and that's neither too soft nor too hard. I want it to give *slightly* when I squeeze it. I find that citrus fruits with the smoothest skins typically produce more juice, but ones with more textured skins work better if you are planning to use a channel knife to spray citrus zest oil on the surface of a cocktail. I avoid any fruit that has soft spots or blemishes on the skin.

In Jeffrey Morgenthaler's *The Bar Book*, the author described his juicing experiments designed to determine whether rolling a piece of citrus on a cutting board or chilling it would increase its juice output. He discovered that the best strategy to maximize juice output was *not* to roll it. He also found that the temperature of the fruit made almost no difference in its juice output. America's Test Kitchen has determined that keeping citrus fruit in the refrigerator, in a sealed plastic bag, will help keep it fresh longer.

On a separate note, some cocktail writers recommend letting freshly squeezed lemon or lime juice age a few hours before using them in a cocktail. They claim this allows the juice to mellow a little. I've tried this technique and find that it results in a cocktail that in fact *is* mellower, but I still miss the bright tartness of fresh-squeezed juice.

# BUILT

# BUILT COCKTAILS

*A "built" cocktail is one that is constructed and chilled in its final serving glass, rather than a mixing glass or cocktail shaker.*

## Three recommendations for making better built cocktails:

1.  Always prechill your glasses, preferably in the freezer for at least 15 minutes. This ensures that your finished cocktail stays chilled longer.

2.  Five of the cocktails in this chapter use either champagne, prosecco, tonic, or club soda. Always prechill these carbonated liquids in the refrigerator for four or more hours. Chilling carbonated liquids produces both colder cocktails and longer-lasting effervescence.

3.  When measuring out carbonated liquid, particularly champagne or prosecco, make sure your jigger is absolutely clean. If any particles exist on the inside of your jigger, they will serve as "nucleation" sites, allowing the carbon dioxide to form bubbles that foam up out of the liquid. This not only makes precise measuring difficult, it also results in a finished cocktail with less effervescence.

*A favorite at
the Cannes
Film Festival*

# BELLINI

*The Bellini is a refreshing, seasonal drink best enjoyed from mid-May to mid-August when fresh peaches are in season. Some writers claim it is the very best champagne cocktail you can make, but that's slightly misleading since it's generally made with Italian prosecco, rather than champagne.*

| | |
|---|---|
| **4 ounces** | **chilled prosecco** *(Zonin Brut Prosecco is both inexpensive and excellent in this drink)* |
| **2 ounces** | **chilled sweetened white peach pureé** *(see p. 27)* |

## Recipe

1. Holding a chilled champagne flute at an angle, gently pour the prosecco down the side of the flute.

2. Add the chilled peach pureé in the same way.

3. Using a barspoon, gently stir once or twice to blend the two ingredients.

## Recipe Notes

The trick to making a Bellini is to combine the two ingredients without having the prosecco erupt in a volcano of foam as it combines with the pureé. When done correctly, the foam will be minimal, and the prosecco will retain most of its effervescence.

Various Bellini recipes call for the ratio of prosecco to peach pureé to be somewhere between 2:1 and 3:1. This recipe uses a 2:1 ratio. If your Bellini has a thicker consistency than you'd like, simply add a little more prosecco.

It's highly important to take time to make your own sweetened white peach pureé for this cocktail. Avoid those bottled or canned Bellini mixes, which never taste as good as the freshly made product. I've even tried using commercially available, frozen white peach pureé, thinking it would be almost as good as fresh. Unfortunately, it's not. Once you try a Bellini made with homemade fresh pureé, you'll never make it any other way.

## History

The Bellini has a particularly heartwarming history. In the 1920s, Harry Pickering, a young scion from a wealthy Bostonian family, took a trip through Europe with his aunt. When they arrived in Venice, they decided to spend a few weeks touring the city, and they frequently enjoyed drinks at the Hotel Europa Bar. The bartender, Giuseppe Cipriani, became friends with young Harry.

And then Harry's aunt departed suddenly without him. One account says she was troubled by his drinking; another claims she ran off with a lover. It turns out that when she left Harry, she left behind her Pekingese dog as well. Thus, the second theory holds, shall we say, a little more water.

Harry's only option was to return to Boston. When he stopped by the Hotel Europa Bar to say goodbye, Giuseppe learned that Harry was short on funds. So he loaned Harry 10,000 lire to help him get home.

Several years later, Harry returned to the Hotel Europa Bar and handed Giuseppe an envelope containing 10,000 lire to repay the loan. And then he handed Giuseppe a second envelope containing an additional 30,000 lire to thank him for his kindness. He suggested that Giuseppe use the money to open his *own* bar, which Giuseppe did, calling it "Harry's Bar." It was there that Giuseppe created the Bellini cocktail, naming it after the Renaissance artist Giovanni Bellini. Harry's Bar in Venice became a popular hangout for the rich and famous, including Truman Capote, Charlie Chaplin, Ernest Hemingway, and Orson Welles.

# Recipe for
## Sweetened White Peach Pureé

| | |
|---|---|
| *1-2* | *white peaches* |
| *1½-3 ounces* | *rich simple syrup* |
| | *(see Chapter 7: Custom-Made Cocktail Syrups)* |

Take one to two white (*not* yellow) peaches at the peak of ripeness and remove the skin with a vegetable peeler (or, if they are particularly ripe, with your fingernails). Hold them over a bowl to catch any juices from this procedure. Remove the pit and drop the remaining peach flesh along with any captured juices into a food processor or blender. Process the peach flesh into a pureé. Strain the liquefied pureé through a strainer to remove any pulp.

Measure the strained peach pureé and add one-half as much *rich* simple syrup (2 parts sugar to 1 part water; see Chapter 7: Custom-Made Cocktail Syrups). For example, the average large white peach will produce about 3 ounces of strained pureé. To this amount, you add 1½ ounces of *rich* simple syrup. Chill the sweetened pureé in the refrigerator, or freeze it for use at a later date.

By using *rich* instead of regular simple syrup, you will end up with more peach and less water in each ounce of pureé. The proper amount of rich simple syrup in this pureé will be determined by both the sweetness of the white peaches and the sweetness of the particular bottle of prosecco you use. As usual, taste and adjust. 🐌

The national
drink of Brazil

# CAIPIRINHA

*Most Americans are unfamiliar with this cocktail and might need a little pronunciation help with both the cocktail and its key ingredient.*

*Caipirinha—the word is Brazilian slang for "a little country girl"—is pronounced:*

**kai-pee-REEN-ya** *(note the emphasis on the third syllable)*

*A Caipirinha is made with Brazilian rum called cachaça, pronounced:*

**ka-SHA-suh** *(note the emphasis on the second syllable)*

*Unlike most rums, which are distilled from molasses, cachaça is distilled from fermented sugarcane juice. This gives cachaça a unique flavor and makes the Caipirinha a nice variation on its cousin, the Daiquiri. Moreover, the Caipirinha adds lime zest oil to further distinguish itself from the Daiquiri.*

| 2 ounces | *Avua Prata Cachaça* |
| | *(Leblon Cachaça is a good alternative )* |
| ¾ ounce | **simple syrup** *(see Chapter 7: Custom-Made* |
| | *Cocktail Syrups)* |
| ½ ounce | **freshly squeezed and strained lime juice** |

## Recipe

1. Using a vegetable peeler, remove the peel from half of a lime.
2. Fill a chilled old fashioned glass with cachaca. Place the peel, green side up, in the bottom of the glass and muddle for 30 seconds to release the lime zest oil.
3. Add ¾ ounce of simple syrup and ½ ounce of strained, freshly squeezed lime juice.
4. Fill the glass with cracked ice and stir to chill.
5. Add a sprig of mint that you've slapped against the back of your hand several times to release its aroma.

## Recipe Notes

Typically, a Caipirinha is constructed by cutting half of a lime into four quarters and muddling them (peel side down) with two teaspoons of granulated sugar in the bottom of an old fashioned glass. Two ounces of cachaça are added, and the glass is filled with cracked ice. This is an easy preparation, but it has a number of problems. The muddling in sugar produces little flavor from the lime zest, and some undiluted sugar always remains in the bottom of the glass. Also, the amount of lime juice in the drink varies from one drink to the next, and you end up with both lime pulp and seeds floating in the cocktail.

The technique I've suggested above is a bit more work than the standard preparation, yet it results in a much better cocktail.

I have a slight preference for Avua Prata Cachaça over Leblon Cachaça, but Leblon might be easier to find.

## History

Two theories have arisen concerning the origin of the Caipirinha. One holds that the drink evolved from a mixture of cachaça, honey, garlic, and lime juice that was used to treat Spanish flu among Brazilian patients during the 1918 pandemic.

A second theory is based on a document discovered in Paraty, a coastal city about 150 miles south of Rio de Janeiro. According to this document, an 1856 cholera epidemic forced people to give up drinking water; instead, they turned to a mixture of *aguardiente* (a sugarcane-based spirit similar to *cachaça*), lime juice, and sugar. That mixture clearly foreshadowed today's Caipirinha.

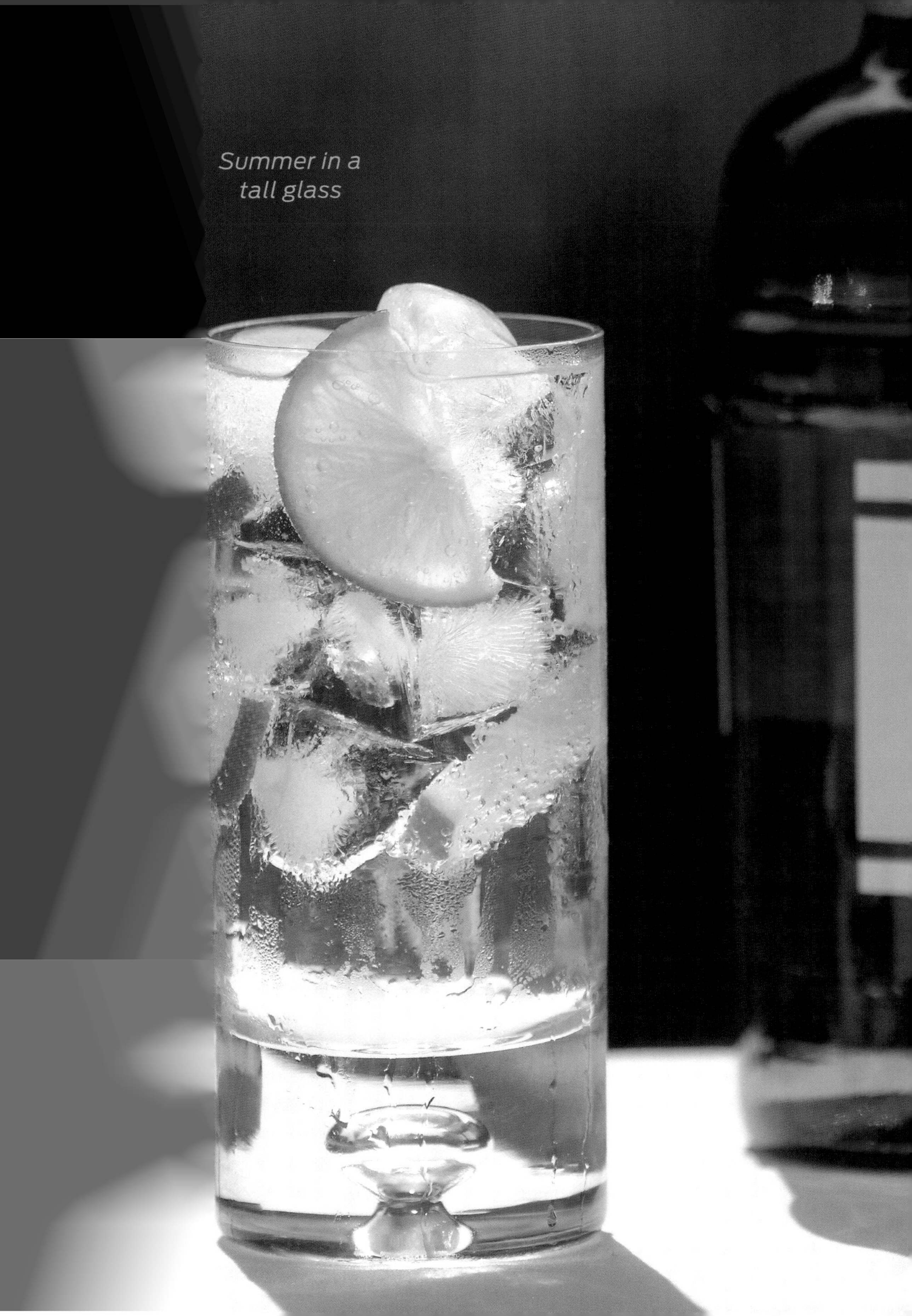
Summer in a
tall glass

# GIN & TONIC

*The Gin & Tonic is a refreshing, warm-weather drink with a history that encompasses both South America and southern Asia. Renowned cocktail writer Toby Cecchini calls it "summer in a tall glass."*

| | |
|---|---|
| *2 ounces* | *Tanqueray London Dry Gin (see recipe notes)* |
| *4–6 ounces* | *chilled Schweppes Tonic Water (see recipe notes)* |
| *2 teaspoons* | *freshly squeezed lime juice* |

## Recipe

1. Fill a large, chilled collins glass three-quarters full of ice cubes.

2. Add the gin and lime juice.

3. Pour the chilled tonic water slowly down the side of the glass. Prechilling the tonic helps to retain the effervescence in the cocktail.

4. Add additional ice cubes to bring the cocktail to just below the rim of the glass.

5. Garnish with half-wheels of lime floating among the ice cubes in the glass.

## Recipe Notes

A Gin & Tonic, like so many cocktails, is an exercise in balance. Respected cocktail writers recommend a gin to tonic ratio of anywhere from 1:1 to 1:3. The danger of a 1:1 ratio is that the drink ends up tasting flat. By contrast, *too* much tonic can lead to a watered-down drink with little gin taste. In the end, the amount of tonic you use comes down to personal taste. But once you have determined your preferred balance, measuring out the tonic, rather than just topping off the glass, is key to creating a consistent cocktail.

The specific brands of gin and tonic you use are also a matter of personal taste. In my opinion, Tanqueray and Schweppes work particularly well together. Plymouth Gin and Fever Tree Gold Label Indian Tonic also make a good pairing if you prefer a gentler drink. Hendrick's Gin also makes an interesting Gin & Tonic if you omit the lime juice and submerge three or four thin-sliced cucumber rounds among the ice cubes as a garnish. The logic of using cucumber is that cucumbers (as well as rose petals) are ingredients used in the production of Hendrick's gin. Hendrick's recommends a ratio of one part gin to three parts tonic. The result is an unusual, but quite nice, version of the Gin & Tonic.

## History

Quinine is the key ingredient in tonic water. For centuries, natives of the Peruvian Andes harvested quinine, an alkaloid, from the bark of the *cinchona* tree and used it to treat the high fever of malaria. They referred to this tree as the "fever tree," a moniker that has been adopted by a current brand of tonic water.

In the 1600s, Spanish missionaries who traveled to Peru learned about the benefits of quinine and took it back to Europe. Its medicinal qualities enabled Europeans to stay well enough to colonize the tropical regions of Africa and Asia.

The English and Dutch soon established large plantations of cinchona trees in both India and Indonesia. By the 1840s, the English were consuming, in India alone, roughly 700 tons of cinchona bark each year. To overcome quinine's inherent bitterness, they mixed it with sugar and water.

In 1858, the first commercial brand of tonic water appeared on the market, and in 1873 Schweppes introduced Indian Quinine Water. It did not take long for the British to add their favorite spirit, gin, to quinine water—thus creating the classic cocktail.

*A great cocktail for large parties and celebrations*

# KIR ROYALE

*You may have already encountered the Kir, a wonderful cocktail made by combining still white wine with the black currant liqueur* crème de cassis. *A Kir Royale is simply a Kir made with sparkling wine. Elegant, light, and easy to prepare, the Kir Royal is perfect for large gatherings.*

| | |
|---|---|
| *4 ounces* | **chilled Gloria Ferrer Sonoma Brut Sparkling Wine** |
| *½ ounce* | **Matilde Crème de Cassis** |

## Recipe

1. Pour the chilled sparkling wine slowly down the side of a chilled champagne flute, to preserve its effervescence.

2. Add the crème de cassis and stir once to blend the two ingredients.

3. Garnish with a lemon twist.

## Recipe Notes

I recommend a brut sparkling wine to offset the sweetness of the Crème de Cassis.

## History

*Crème de cassis* dates back at least to 1841. It was later mixed with white wine to make what was then known as a Blanc Cassis.

When the Germans invaded France in World War II, they shipped all the good French wine back to Germany, leaving only low-quality wine for the embattled French. After the war, a man named Felix Kir, the mayor of Dijon and a former resistance fighter who helped liberate more than 5,000 allied prisoners of war from a nearby German camp, suggested to his compatriots that the remaining low-quality wine be consumed as Blanc Cassis cocktails. That suggestion was so well received that the cocktail was renamed in honor of the new mayor and resistance hero.

*The best of Southern
plantation living*

# MINT JULEP

*One Kentucky legend has it that if you sip a really well-made Mint Julep, you might hear angels sing! Even if you don't experience that phenomenon, a Mint Julep with the right mint and bourbon can be an exceptional drink.*

| | |
|---|---|
| *3 ounces* | ***Basil Hayden Bourbon*** |
| *18 large leaves* | ***fresh spearmint*** |
| *½ ounce* | ***mint syrup*** *(see recipe for mint syrup in Chapter 7: Custom-Made Cocktail Syrups)* |

## Recipe

1. Combine the bourbon and mint leaves in a julep cup or small collins glass and gently muddle the mint leaves until they are bruised, but not broken into pieces.

2. Allow this mixture to marinate for roughly seven minutes to infuse the mint flavor into the bourbon.

3. Add ½ ounce of mint simple syrup to the mint-infused bourbon without removing the mint leaves.

4. Taste and add more mint simple syrup if you prefer a sweeter drink.

5. Fill the julep cup with crushed ice. To crush ice, most bartenders use a traditional canvas bag called a Lewis Bag. For more information, see the discussion of Lewis Bags in Chapter 8: Recommended Bar Equipment.

6. Stir the mixture for 15 to 20 seconds to chill the drink.

7. Add more crushed ice to the cup as necessary so that it mounds slightly above the lip of the cup.

8. Slap about three bushy sprigs of spearmint against the back of your hand several times to bruise the leaves and release the aroma.

9. Stick these sprigs into the ice to form a garnish on one side of the cup.

10. Insert a paper or stainless steel straw among the spearmint leaves. The placement of the straw near the mint garnish allows the aroma from the leaves to enhance the overall taste of the drink as you sip from the straw. Serve and enjoy.

## Recipe Notes

Mint syrup is an old Southern secret to making a really fine Mint Julep.

Most recipe books recommend getting the freshest mint available. Teddy Roosevelt was such a fan of Mint Juleps that he planted a mint garden on the White House grounds.

A spearmint highly prized for making Mint Juleps is the variety known as Kentucky Colonel. However, the chance of finding that variety at your local produce market is fairly remote. If you're a genuine fan of Mint Juleps, you might want to follow Teddy Roosevelt's example and start a Kentucky Colonel spearmint container garden. You'll find this variety also works well in Mojitos. See the mint syrup recipe in Chapter 7: Custom-Made Cocktail Syrups, for two sources of live Kentucky Colonel mint plants.

## History

One of the most knowledgeable authorities on the Mint Julep is Richard Harwell. In his book, *The Mint Julep*, Harwell writes that the cocktail was first created in Virginia, but that early julep was a far cry from our current version. It consisted of a blend of brandies, according to the writings of British naval officer Frederick Marryat who visited Virginia in the 1830s.

The Mint Julep soon became an upper-class drink associated with plantation living, since plantations usually had the ice houses that made the cocktail possible in summer months. And since that period, many interesting tales have been spun about the drink.

For instance, in 1842 Charles Dickens was touring the States and is said to have dined with Washington Irving in a Baltimore hotel, when an admirer sent over a Mint Julep served in a large bowl surrounded by flowers. The two writers punctuated their conversation by taking turns leaning over the bowl sipping the drink through straws.

In 1845, a southerner named Trapler traveled to Oxford University in England and introduced his hosts to the Mint Julep. They were obviously impressed, because ever since then Oxford has celebrated the first day in June as Mint Julep Day.

After the Civil War, as brandy became less affordable to the vanquished Southerners, they switched to bourbon as their base spirit for juleps. When journalist H. L. Mencken suggested rye whiskey might also be a good choice, Irvin S. Cobb, a fellow writer and former Kentuckian, responded: "Any guy who'd put rye in a Mint Julep ... would put scorpions in a baby's bed."

*Evolved from the world's oldest cocktail, El Draque*

# MOJITO

*A well-made Mojito is a memorable warm-weather cocktail. Unfortunately, most Mojitos served in bars are overdiluted and lack sufficient rum and mint flavors. The recipe below overcomes these issues.*

| | |
|---|---|
| *2½ ounces* | **Mount Gay Eclipse Rum** |
| *18 mint leaves* | **medium to large fresh spearmint leaves** |
| *1 ounce* | **freshly squeezed lime juice** |
| *1 ounce* | **mint syrup** (see the recipe for mint syrup in Chapter 7: Custom-Made Cocktail Syrups) |
| *3 ounces* | **chilled Schweppes Club Soda** |
| *1 dash* | **Angostura Bitters** (optional; see recipe notes) |

## Recipe

1.  Combine the rum and spearmint leaves in a chilled collins glass. Gently muddle until the leaves are bruised, but not broken into pieces. Allow this mixture to marinate for seven minutes.

2.  Add the fresh lime juice and mint simple syrup.

3.  Fill the glass with ice cubes and add 3 ounces of chilled club soda.

4.  Stir just enough to incorporate the club soda into the rest of the drink. Taste and add more club soda if desired.

5.  Take the two halves of the lime you squeezed for juice and push them down into the drink for a colorful garnish.

6.  Slap several bushy sprigs of spearmint against the back of your hand several times to bruise the leaves and release their aroma. Stick these sprigs into the ice near the rim of the glass.

## Recipe Notes

This recipe calls for an amber rum—Mount Gay Eclipse—instead of the traditional white or light rum used in most recipes. That will result in more rum flavor in your finished drink.

To achieve greater mint flavor, the recipe calls for mint simple syrup instead of the regular simple syrup or sugar, and also suggests that the spearmint leaves be infused in the rum. Note that you want *only* the mint and the rum together in the infusion process.

Prechilling the club soda will help retain its effervescence in the cocktail.

To avoid overdiluting the cocktail, the recipe uses ice cubes, rather than crushed or cracked ice, to chill the drink. Moreover, while many recipes call for "topping off" the drink with club soda (which by itself can also contribute to overdilution), this recipe recommends adding a measured three ounces of club soda in the glass. If the level of the finished drink ends up dramatically below the rim of the glass, consider adding more ice cubes instead of more club soda.

A few cocktail writers recommend using a dash or two of Angostura Bitters in a Mojito. This makes a nice alternative to a regular Mojito, but try this recipe first *without* the bitters.

## History

In Chapter 1, I noted that Sir Francis Drake combated scurvy during his explorations of the New World in the late 1500s by adopting a native drink made with limes, mint, sugarcane juice, and *aguardiente* (a primitive, sugarcane-based rum). Caribbean settlers referred to this cocktail as *El Draque*.

Some sources say that after the Bacardi family started producing rum in Cuba in 1862, rum replaced *aguardiente,* and *El Draque* became the Mojito. Since this was a minor substitution of a closely related spirit, it can reasonably be argued that the Mojito is in fact the world's oldest "cocktail."

The Mojito was one of Ernest Hemingway's favorite cocktails. He regularly enjoyed this cocktail at La Bodeguita del Medio bar in Havana during his years in Cuba.

*The most popular version is made with Aperol*

# VENETIAN SPRITZ

*The Venetian Spritz is a light cocktail that tradition-ally combines prosecco with sparkling water and one of several bitter Italian aperitifs, such as Cynar, Campari, Cappelletti, or Aperol. Having experimented with all four of these aperitifs, I prefer Aperol in this drink.*

*The Aperol Spritz sometimes comes under criticism for being too sweet. The recipe below increases the prosecco, omits the sparkling water, and adds lemon juice, all of which serve to overcome the sweetness and add complex-ity to the drink, making it a lovely cocktail for a summer evening.*

| | |
|---|---|
| **4 ounces** | **chilled brut prosecco** *(Zonin Brut Prosecco is a fine and inexpensive choice)* |
| **2 ounces** | **Aperol** |
| **2 teaspoons** | **freshly squeezed lemon juice** *(see recipe notes)* |

## Recipe

1. Pour the chilled prosecco slowly down the side of a chilled wine glass or champagne flute to retain its effervescence.

2. Add the Aperol, again pouring gently down the side of the glass.

3. Add the lemon juice and stir briefly.

4. Insert one or two half-slices of orange into the drink. This visual and flavor garnish greatly enhances the cocktail.

5. Add enough ice cubes to bring the liquid to just below the rim of the glass.

## Recipe Notes

Always add the lemon juice last to reduce the loss of the prosecco's effervescence. If you add it before the prosecco, the prosecco will erupt in a volcano of fizz. I also recommend washing your jigger thoroughly to remove any tiny particles clinging to the inside of the jigger that could act as nucleation sites for bubbles, causing the prosecco to foam up and make accurate measurement difficult.

## History

In 1815, Austria annexed into the Austrian Empire a section of Italy that included Venice. When Austrian soldiers, who were stationed in the new territory, found the local Italian wines too strong in flavor, they begin to add water to the wine to lighten the taste. Later, carbonated water replaced still water, and a drink akin to today's wine spritzer was born. Eventually, various Italian aperitifs were added to the drink, creating the Venetian Spritz.

Aperol became the popular aperitif in this drink during the 1950s; and, according to Jim Meehan in *Meehan's Bartenders Manual*, prosecco replaced the still wine in the 1990s. By 2021, *Drinks International* ranked the Aperol Spritz as the ninth best-selling cocktail in the world.

## Cocktail Tip:

### When building a cocktail, add the cheaper ingredients first.

Add ingredients such as simple syrup and citrus juice to your shaker or mixing glass *before* you add the alcohol. The reason for this is self-evident. These ingredients cost a fraction of what alcoholic spirits cost. So if you make a mistake adding one of these less-expensive ingredients, you can simply throw out the batch and start over without wasting a lot of money. ❧

*A refreshing offshoot
of the Mint Julep*

# WHISKEY SMASH

*The Whiskey Smash gets little coverage from cocktail writers, though it can be a nice addition to your repertoire. Closely related to the Mint Julep, it incorporates elements of the Old Fashioned and Whiskey Sour.*

| | |
|---|---|
| *2 ounces* | **Basil Hayden Bourbon** |
| *2 teaspoons* | **freshly squeezed lemon juice** |
| *1 tablespoon* | **mint simple syrup** (see recipe in Chapter 7: Custom-Made Cocktail Syrups) |
| *8 leaves* | **fresh spearmint, medium to large in size** |
| *lemon skins* | **lemon skins peeled from half of a lemon** |

## Recipe

1. Using a vegetable peeler, peel the outer skin from half of a standard-size lemon. Try to peel only the yellow part, leaving the bitter white pith attached to the lemon.

2. Squeeze the skinned lemon and set aside the fresh juice.

3. Place the peels, yellow side up, in a chilled old fashioned glass.

4. Add the bourbon and muddle the peels for about 30 seconds.

5. Add the mint leaves, and muddle again for 30 seconds.

6. Add the mint simple syrup and the lemon juice.

7. Fill the glass with cracked ice and stir about 25 times to chill and dilute the cocktail.

8. Garnish with a sprig of spearmint that you've whipped against the back of your hand to release its aroma.

## Recipe Notes

Most Whiskey Smash recipes direct you to cut a quarter of a lemon into several pieces and muddle them together with the mint leaves. When I did this, I ended up with a drink that not only was too sour but also had little of the wonderful flavor of lemon zest oil. So I developed the technique above, which results in the right amount of lemon juice plus a very nice nuance of lemon zest oil.

Some recipes call for this cocktail to be shaken, but I strongly prefer it as a built drink.

## History

Smashes, which were very popular in the 1800s, were made not just with whiskey, but also with gin, rum, brandy, and even scotch. A recipe for the Whiskey Smash first appeared in Harry Johnson's 1888 book *New and Improved Bartender's Manual, or How to Mix Drinks in the Present Style.*

# CHAPTER 4

# STIRRED

# STIRRED COCKTAILS

*Ignore James Bond. He's famous for ordering his Martinis "shaken, not stirred." Bond might have been the epitome of sophistication on a number of subjects, but unfortunately not on Martinis. In this section I'll cover the reasons that Martinis and select other cocktails should always be stirred.*

As a class, stirred cocktails are preferred by more-seasoned and more-sophisticated drinkers than are built cocktails. They also require more skill to prepare.

Stirred cocktails are a mixture of alcoholic ingredients—base spirits, vermouth or other fortified wines, bitters, and/or bitter aperitifs. Generally, the only nonalcoholic ingredient in a stirred cocktail is sugar or a sugar-based syrup.

One of the joys of a properly made stirred cocktail, such as the Martini or a Manhattan, is its thick, almost viscous quality—something that Kevin Liu, in his book *Craft Cocktails at Home*, refers to as mouthfeel. A stirred cocktail is often beautifully translucent in the glass, sometimes resembling a pane of stained glass. And a stirred cocktail tends to have a stronger flavor, which is why these drinks often appeal to more-sophisticated drinkers.

Stirred cocktails are assembled in a mixing glass with ice, and stirred with a barspoon. The goal of stirring the cocktail with ice is twofold. First, you want to reduce the temperature of the drink to between 19°F and 31°F, depending on your personal preference. Second, you want the melting ice to dilute the drink a bit. Stirring cocktails properly with a barspoon requires some practice; the proper technique is covered in this section.

## Recommendations for making better stirred cocktails:

1. Always prechill your mixing and serving glasses in the freezer for 15 minutes or more. This will ensure that your finished cocktail is properly chilled and stays chilled longer.

2. Assemble all the ingredients in a mixing glass.

3. Fill the mixing glass with ice cubes until the level of the liquid is roughly one inch below the rim of the glass. Any clearance less than one inch can result in both ice and liquid flying out of the mixing glass and onto your bar mat (or your shirt) as you rapidly stir the cocktail.

4. Some writers suggest using a mixture of one-half ice cubes and one-half cracked ice to achieve a lower temperature in a stirred cocktail. I've tried this technique. The finished drink is in fact colder, but it sometimes can be a little too diluted for my taste. I recommend using only ice cubes. If the finished cocktail is not quite as cold as you like, consider superchilling it as described in guideline #6 of Chapter 2: Guidelines for Great Cocktails.

## Technique for using a barspoon to stir cocktails in a mixing glass

1. After you've filled the mixing glass with ingredients and ice cubes, slide the barspoon down the inside of the mixing glass until the lip of the spoon bowl rests on the bottom of the mixing glass.

2. Position the spoon bowl so the bottom (convex side) is touching the side of the glass.

3. Hold the exposed shaft between the thumb and first knuckle of your index finger (see photo on opposite page).

4. Now position the lower portion of the shaft between the first knuckles of your third and fourth fingers.

5. Looking down at the mixing glass from above, imagine that the top of the glass is a clock face with the part of the glass closest to you being the 6 o'clock position. Starting with the shaft of the barspoon at the 6 o'clock position on the mixing glass rim, use your ring finger to push the bowl of the

barspoon around the inside of the bottom of the glass clockwise to the 12 o'clock position on the rim. Remember to keep the bottom (convex side) of the spoon bowl touching the side of the mixing glass.

6. When the shaft reaches the 12 o'clock position, stop pushing with your ring finger and start pulling with your middle finger so that the barspoon continues clockwise around the mixing glass until it gets back to the 6 o'clock position.

7. Repeat steps 5 and 6. As you stir, try to isolate all the stirring motions in your fingers and wrist. You want to avoid moving your entire arm. A good way to accomplish this is to keep your elbow pressed against your side.

8. Target rotating the barspoon on the inside of the mixing glass 80 times in 25 seconds. At the end of 25 seconds, your cocktail should be both properly chilled and diluted. Remove the barspoon.

9. Strain the chilled drink into a cocktail glass. In the U.S., a julep strainer is traditionally used to strain a stirred cocktail. If you do not have a julep strainer, a Hawthorne strainer is a fine substitute. Most of the world uses Hawthorne strainers to strain both stirred and shaken drinks.

10. Practice your stirring technique with a mixture of water and ice cubes in a mixing glass until you become proficient. The more you practice, the more proficient you'll become—and stirring proficiency is one mark of a good bartender.

*Made with Campari, an Italian aperitif worth getting to know*

# BOULEVARDIER

This is a superb cocktail that was all but forgotten until Ted Haigh resurrected it in 2009 in his excellent book *Vintage Spirits and Forgotten Cocktails*. It is now much better known, and, like its fellow classic cocktails the Clover Club and the Pegu Club, the Boulevardier even has a bar named after it.

Some writers argue that the Boulevardier is simply a Negroni made with bourbon instead of gin—but that's an oversimplification. I side with other writers who view it as a variation on a Manhattan, one in which Campari—a bitter Italian aperitif—replaces the Manhattan's Angostura Bitters. I prefer the Boulevardier over the Manhattan, as the Campari and bourbon in the Boulevardier work particularly well to smooth out each other's rough edges.

Campari is an acquired taste for most people. According to Gary Regan, the citizens of Milan believe that you must try Campari at least three times before you enjoy it. I've grown to love Campari in Boulevardiers, in Negronis, and even by itself on the rocks. So don't give up on this cocktail after just one sip.

| 2 ounces | **bourbon** (*see recipe notes below*) |
| 1 ounce | **Carpano Antica Formula Italian Sweet Vermouth** |
| 1 ounce | **Campari** |

## Recipe

1. Combine the ingredients in a chilled mixing glass. Add ice cubes and stir until cold.

2. Strain into a chilled martini glass.

3. Cut a six-inch strip of lemon peel with a channel knife, allowing the zest oil to spray onto the surface of the cocktail.

4. Twist the strip into a corkscrew around the handle of your barspoon and slide it off the end. You now have a proverbial citrus twist.

5. Hang one end of the twist over the rim of the glass as a visual garnish. Let the other end drift into the cocktail where it will add a little more flavor to the drink.

6. Consider adding a Tillen Farms Merry Maraschino Cherry as an additional garnish.

## Recipe Notes

The bourbon you choose to use in this recipe matters. 1792 Bourbon makes a smooth Boulevardier, while Basil Hayden and Elijah Craig bourbons result in a slightly bolder-tasting cocktail. For special occasions, Jefferson Reserve, Very Old, Very Small Batch Bourbon is a pricey, but superb, choice.

The addition of lemon zest oil elevates the Boulevardier from being a good cocktail to being a great one.

The Boulevardier lends itself well to superchilling. Simply place the finished cocktail in the freezer for roughly 15 minutes until its temperature drops down to about 19°F. Now you're approaching what the ancients referred to as "nectar of the gods." It really is that good!

## History

The Boulevardier was created in the 1920s at Harry's New York Bar in Paris. The bar was owned by Harry McElhone, who worked at New York's Plaza Hotel bar before Prohibition. Harry's Bar became popular with many celebrities, including Ernest Hemingway, Sinclair Lewis, and F. Scott Fitzgerald. Erskine Gwynne, who was a member of the Vanderbilt family, was another regular. Gwynne published the English-language literary magazine *Boulevardier* for American expatriates living in Paris. In his book, *Barflies and Cocktails,* Harry McElhone wrote that Gwynne suggested the recipe for the Boulevardier, which explains the name of the cocktail. Gwynne also published a novel, *Paris Pandemonium,* before returning to the United States. In 1938, complications from a serious car accident left him paralyzed until his death 10 years later. Gwynne will be remembered not so much for his magazine or novel as for the remarkable cocktail he helped create.

On a related note, in 1928 George Gershwin used a piano in Harry's downstairs bar to compose *An American in Paris.* I like to think that Erskine Gwynne might have been enjoying a Boulevardier upstairs as Gershwin worked on his composition.

*One of the few classic cocktails made with Irish whiskey*

# EMERALD

*A cousin of the Manhattan, the Emerald calls for Irish whiskey and orange bitters in place of the Manhattan's bourbon (or rye) and Angostura Bitters. These two substitutions make the Emerald smoother than most Manhattans.*

*Note: Some contemporary Emerald recipes call for gin mixed with one of several green-colored liqueurs, giving the cocktail a distinctive green hue. But the classic Emerald cocktail is actually brown in color. Its name is derived from Ireland's nickname—the "Emerald Isle."*

| | |
|---|---|
| *2 ounces* | *Irish whiskey* |
| *1 ounce* | *Carpano Antica Formula Italian Sweet Vermouth* |

## Recipe

1. Combine ingredients in a chilled mixing glass. Add ice cubes and stir until cold.

2. Strain into a chilled martini glass.

3. Cut a five-inch strip of orange peel with a channel knife to spray zest oil over the surface of the cocktail.

4. Twist the orange peel into a corkscrew around the handle of your barspoon and slide it off the end. You now have the proverbial citrus twist.

5. Hang one end of the twist over the rim of the glass as a visual garnish. Let the other end drift into the cocktail where it will add a little more flavor to the drink.

6. Add a Tillen Farms Merry Maraschino Cherry as an additional garnish.

## Recipe Notes

Tullamore D.E.W. Irish Whiskey makes a nice Emerald, but for special occasions, Red-breast 12 Year Irish Whiskey is wonderful.

Most Emerald recipes call for orange bitters, but I prefer the addition of orange zest oil to the surface of the cocktail. It provides just the right amount of orange flavor to bring out the best in the whiskey, particularly when using Redbreast.

If you replace the Irish whiskey in the above recipe with scotch, you have another classic cocktail—the Rob Roy.

## History

Unfortunately, little documentation can be found concerning the origin of the Emerald. We know its close cousin the Rob Roy was created in 1894 by a bartender at New York's Waldorf Astoria to celebrate the opening of a musical about the Scottish hero Rob Roy Macgregor. It's possible that the same bartender substituted Irish whiskey for the Scotch whisky in a Rob Roy, thus creating the Emerald cocktail.

## Cocktail Tip:

### Don't store base spirits in the refrigerator.

A key to achieving balance in a cocktail is to control the dilution from ice as it melts in your shaker or mixing glass. If you use chilled base spirits, ice will not melt as quickly, which means your finished cocktail may taste overly strong. ❧

*The likely forerunner
of all classic stirred
cocktails*

# MANHATTAN

*In his* Joy of Mixology, *Gary Regan describes the Manhattan as the finest cocktail on earth. And in his book* Esquire Drinks, *David Wondrich claims that a properly made Manhattan is the only cocktail that can hold its own against the Martini.*

*With only three ingredients, this cocktail is fairly simple to make. The skill lies in matching a good-quality whiskey with a compatible vermouth in a ratio that allows each to complement the other.*

*Some cocktail writers point out that the area code for Manhattan (212) also happens to be an excellent guide for making a Manhattan cocktail.*

| | |
|---|---|
| *2 ounces* | **rye or bourbon** *(see recipe notes below)* |
| *1 ounces* | **Carpano Antica Formula Italian Sweet Vermouth** |
| *2 dashes* | **Angostura Bitters** *(2 dashes equal ¼ teaspoon)* |

## Recipe

1. Combine all ingredients in a chilled mixing glass. Add ice cubes and stir until cold.
2. Strain into a chilled martini glass.
3. Garnish with Tillen Farms Merry Maraschino cherries.

## Recipe Notes

At various times in the history of this drink, three different classes of whiskey have reigned supreme. Prior to Prohibition, rye was the whiskey of choice. During that "dry era" in the United States, imported (smuggled-in) Canadian whisky was the only option. And after Prohibition ended, bourbon became the spirit of choice. However, rye is now making a strong comeback.

Since rye was the first whiskey used in a Manhattan, it is a perfectly good option. Crown Royal Northern Harvest Rye makes a very tasty rye Manhattan. Add a little lemon zest oil on the surface of this version and you have an even more special cocktail.

However, as Gary Regan writes, there is nothing wrong with using bourbon in your Manhattan if you prefer it to rye. Both 1792 and Basil Hayden bourbons are good options. For very special occasions, Jefferson Reserve Very Old Very Small Batch Bourbon is also quite enjoyable. I prefer bourbon Manhattans made without added citrus zest oil on the surface of the cocktail.

If you are serving novice whiskey drinkers, a time-honored strategy to help them learn to appreciate the Manhattan is to add to the cocktail a half-teaspoon (or slightly more) of sweetened, cherry-flavored syrup from a bottle of Tillen Farms Merry Maraschino Cherries.

Consider superchilling your Manhattan by placing it in the freezer for roughly 15 minutes until the temperature drops to 19°F. This smooths out the rough edges and makes all the flavors a little more enjoyable.

## History

One popular theory for the origin of the Manhattan is that it was created at the Manhattan Club in New York City on November 4, 1874, during an event thrown by Winston Churchill's American-born mother, Jennie Jerome, in honor of Samuel Tilden's election as governor of New York. However, reliable sources argue that Jennie Jerome was actually in Europe at that time, pregnant with Winston. Her son was born late that month at Blenheim Palace in England.

A second theory holds that the cocktail was created at the Manhattan Club—but not at an event hosted by Winston Churchill's mother.

And a third theory, promoted in the 1880s by William Mulhall, a bartender at New York's Hoffman House, claims that a certain "Mr. Black" created the Manhattan in the 1860s at a nearby bar on Broadway.

The only common thread these stories share is that the Manhattan was created on the island of Manhattan sometime in the 1860s or '70s. By the 1880s it had become an extremely popular drink.

It is said that the legendary New York banker J. P. Morgan enjoyed a Manhattan at the end of every business day at the Waldorf Astoria Bar.

## Cocktail Tip:

### *Use top-quality maraschino cherries in your cocktails.*

I've never cared for the flavor of many popular brands of maraschino cherries. They often contain high-fructose corn syrup, artificial red dyes, artificial flavoring, and preservatives.

Some people swear by Luxardo Original Maraschino Cherries, which are imported from Italy. These are marasca cherries preserved in their own syrup without artificial coloring or flavoring. They're expensive, and to me they taste heavy. There's nothing subtle about them, yet they have a lot of fans.

My favorite cocktail cherries are Tillen Farms Merry Maraschino Cherries from Stonewall Kitchens. Like Luxardo, these cherries contain no artificial dyes or preservative— and they're less than half the price. Moreover, the syrup they're packed in is made with cane sugar rather than high-fructose corn syrup. It has a nice flavor, and a spoonful can be a mellowing factor in select cocktails such as the Manhattan. I find the most reliable source of these cherries is Amazon. One note of caution: Tillen Farms offers several varieties of cherries. I recommend its Merry Maraschinos for cocktails, rather than its Bourbon Bada Bing or its Fire & Spiced varieties. 🍒

*The epitome of elegance and sophistication*

# MARTINI

*Hollywood certainly deserves some credit for the Martini's image. The* Thin Man *films, which debuted in 1934, featured two amusing detectives—Nick and Nora—who enjoyed Martinis throughout the series. Cary Grant and Deborah Kerr sipped Martinis in* An Affair to Remember. *And James Bond, the epitome of sophistication himself, consumed Martinis in several "007" movies. However, Bond created some confusion among connoisseurs by insisting that his Martinis be "shaken, not stirred."*

*Another reason for its sophisticated image is that the Martini made with gin is not easily appreciated by novice drinkers. Like the Boulevardier, the Negroni, and the Manhattan, the Martini is an acquired taste.*

| | |
|---|---|
| 2¼ ounces | Plymouth Gin |
| ¾ ounce | Dolin Dry Vermouth |

## Recipe

1. Combine the ingredients in a chilled mixing glass. Add ice cubes and stir until cold.

2. Strain into a chilled martini glass.

3. Cut a four-inch strip of lemon peel with a channel knife to spray zest oil onto the surface of this cocktail.

4. Twist the strip into a corkscrew around the handle of your barspoon and slide it off the end. You now have a proverbial citrus twist.

5. Hang one end over the rim of the glass as a visual garnish. Let the other end drift into the cocktail where it will add a little more flavor to the drink.

6. Place the finished cocktail in the freezer for roughly 15 minutes until the temperature reaches about 19°F.

## Recipe Notes

If you prefer an olive in your martini, omit the lemon zest. Adding a little olive brine makes the cocktail a Dirty Martini.

And substituting pickled onion for the olive makes the cocktail a Gibson.

Plymouth Gin was often called for in early Martini recipes and it is still an excellent choice. The proper ratio of gin to vermouth is one of the most hotly contested issues of the last century. The 3:1 ratio of gin to vermouth in this recipe, sometimes called a Nick and Nora Martini, is a great starting point for experimentation. A Martini with a low ratio of gin to vermouth, like the Nick and Nora, is referred to as a Wet Martini. More-seasoned drinkers often prefer a drier Martini—a ratio of 5:1 or even 7:1. It is simply a matter of personal taste. Legend has it that Ernest Hemingway himself favored an astonishing 15:1 ratio, which he referred to as a Montgomery Martini, because during World War II the English Field Marshal Montgomery is said to have preferred to attack only when the odds were "15 to 1" in his favor.

Since the Gin Martini is simply gin and vermouth, there is little to mask the taste of poor-quality spirits, so do use high-quality liquors. Plymouth Gin is one of the finest and smoothest gins you can use in any drink, and it is especially good in a Martini. Dolin Dry Vermouth is also excellent. Note, however, that Dolin also offers Dolin Blanc Vermouth. Both are French vermouths, but Dolin Blanc is slightly sweeter than Dolin Dry and makes a somewhat gentler Martini. While sophisticated Martini drinkers will probably prefer a Martini made with Dolin Dry, drinkers who are new to the Martini are likely to prefer Dolin Blanc.

In the early 1900s, the recipe for the Martini often included a dash or two of orange bitters. The use of orange bitters continued well into the 1930s, after which it disappeared for several decades, only to reappear in recent years. I suggest trying a Martini *without* bitters first, but at least once you should try a Gin Martini made with a dash of Fee Brothers Orange Bitters.

*Note:* Vodka Martinis have become increasingly popular in the last 60 years. The recipe is easy. Simply substitute vodka for the gin, and use a lemon twist as a garnish. Since most vodkas are less assertive than gin, consider starting with a ratio of 4 to 6 portions of vodka to 1 portion of vermouth.

## History

Conflicting theories abound concerning the origin of the Martini. One theory proposes that a man on his way to Martinez, California, stopped at Jerry Thomas's bar in San Francisco and asked Thomas to make him a new cocktail. Thomas complied, and when the customer asked the name of the drink, he dubbed it a "Martinez," in honor of the customer's destination. Thomas's recipe, which was published in the 1887 edition of his *Bar-Tender's Guide,* blends Old Tom Gin (a sweet gin) with Italian sweet vermouth, a dash of Boker's bitters, and two dashes of maraschino liqueur. This combination would result in a somewhat sweet cocktail, with little resemblance to our current dry Martini.

A second theory argues that a gold miner challenged a bartender named Julio Richelieu, of Martinez, to make him something special. Unlike Thomas's creation, no record of ingredients for Richelieu's cocktail exists, but Richelieu apparently named the cocktail a Martinez.

The Martinez cocktail is still around today, with ingredients that generally follow Jerry Thomas's recipe. So, while the people of San Francisco and Martinez can argue about who created the Martinez, the Martinez is *not* the Martini. Nonetheless, the citizens of Martinez in 1992 erected a brass plaque proclaiming their town the actual birthplace of the Martini.

A third theory proposes that in 1911 a bartender at New York's Knickerbocker Hotel made a drink featuring gin and dry vermouth for the oil baron John D. Rockefeller. The bartender, named Martini di Arma di Taggia, named the drink after himself. It is said that Rockefeller was so impressed with the cocktail that he introduced it to all his friends.

However, there are two problems with this theory: Rockefeller was in fact a teetotaler; and a recipe for the Dry Martini appeared five years earlier in *Louis' Mixed Drinks with Hints for the Care and Serving of Wines,* by Louis Muckensturm. That writer's Martini called for a two-to-one ratio of dry gin to French vermouth, two dashes of orange bitters, and a dash of Curaçao. We may never know who actually created the Martini, but Muckensturm seems to have been the first to publish a recipe that's similar to today's cocktail.

Many legends continue to surround the Martini. One of my favorites is that after signing legislation to repeal Prohibition in 1933, President Franklin D. Roosevelt proceeded to mix the first legal Martini in almost 14 years. Another legend has it that during the liberation of Paris in 1945, Ernest Hemingway led 10 "Free French" soldiers into the Ritz Hotel bar to "liberate" it and ordered multiple rounds of Martinis for the soldiers.

Among the many books on the history of the Martini, two are particularly worthwhile: *The Martini* by Barnaby Conrad III, and *The Martini Companion* by Gary and Mardee Regan.

## Cocktail Tip:

*Use either one or three olives as a garnish in a Martini, not two.*

It is considered "bad luck," and thus bad form, to use two olives as a garnish in a Martini. I've adopted the same protocol for cherries in those cocktails that call for cherry garnishes. 🍒

A cocktail beloved
by professional
bartenders

# NEGRONI

*Jason Kosmas and Dushan Zaric, coauthors of Speak-easy, refer to the Negroni as the "Mrs. Robinson of cocktails"—a reference to the 1967 film The Graduate, since it's the cocktail with which so many bartenders end up having an affair.*

*Because the Negroni includes Campari, it usually appeals to someone with a sophisticated palate. As mentioned earlier, the citizens of Milan are said to believe that you must try Campari at least three times before you enjoy it—so don't reject a Negroni based on just one sip.*

| | |
|---|---|
| *1–2 ounces* | *Tanqueray Gin (see recipe notes below)* |
| *1 ounce* | *Carpano Antica Formula Italian Sweet Vermouth* |
| *1 ounce* | *Campari* |

## Recipe

1. Combine all ingredients in a chilled mixing glass. Add ice cubes and stir until cold.

2. Strain into a chilled martini glass.

3. Cut a five-inch strip of orange peel with a channel knife, allowing the orange zest oil to spray onto the surface of the cocktail.

4. Twist the strip into a corkscrew around the handle of your barspoon and slide it off the end. You now have a proverbial citrus twist.

5. Hang one end of the twist over the rim of the glass as a visual garnish. Let the other end drift into the cocktail where it will add a little more flavor to the drink.

## Recipe Notes

The classic Negroni recipe calls for one ounce each of gin, vermouth, and Campari. The combination makes a very good cocktail, particularly for those who are new to a Negroni. However, Stanley Tucci, the actor, TV travel host, and a gourmet of Italian descent, recommends doubling the volume of gin—which takes this cocktail to a new level. Try it both ways and see which you prefer.

The recipe above departs from Tucci's Negroni in two important ways. First, it uses the traditional technique of stirring this cocktail, whereas Tucci shakes his drink. Second, it adds orange zest oil to the surface of the cocktail. Tucci garnishes his own Negroni with a slice of orange.

*Note:* Most Italians prefer their Negronis on the rocks.

## History

The Negroni has much in common with the Boulevardier. They both feature sweet vermouth and Campari; and they both were created as a result of a customer's suggestion, rather than through innovation on the part of a bartender. The generally accepted account of the Negroni's origin sets the scene in 1919. At the Caffè Casoni in Florence, an Italian count named Camillo Negroni asked bartender Fosco Scarselli to modify an Americano cocktail—a drink consisting of Campari, sweet vermouth, and club soda—by substituting gin for the club soda. The new cocktail, which became a tremendous success, was named for Negroni himself, conveying on him a measure of immortality.

It is completely believable that Count Negroni might have wanted a drink with more substance than the Americano. In spite of his aristocratic roots, Negroni was an adventurer who spent time in the American West as both a gambler and a cowboy.

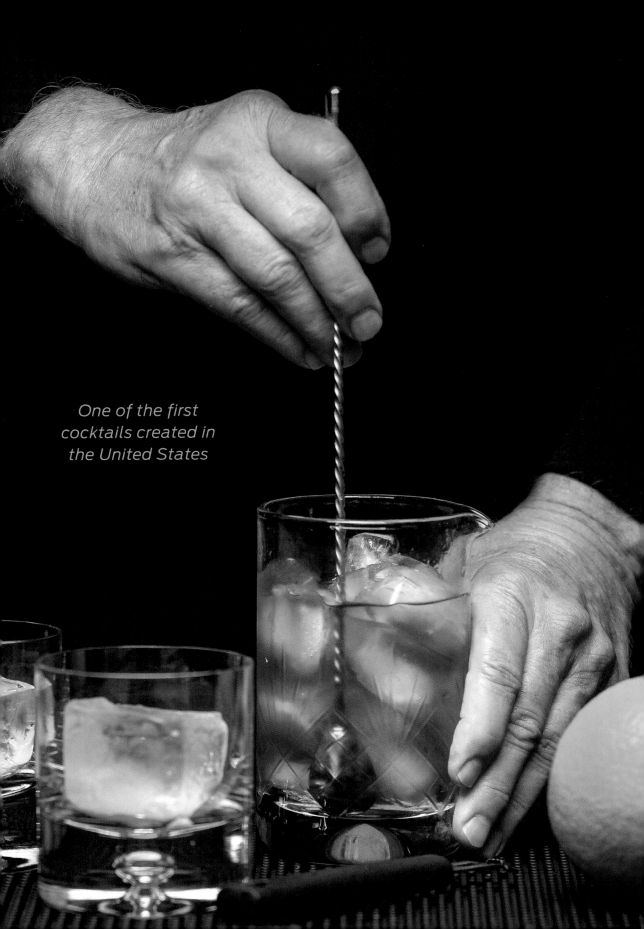

*One of the first cocktails created in the United States*

# OLD FASHIONED

*Typically ranked among the top five classic cocktails, the Old Fashioned has enjoyed a surge in popularity since being featured in the television series* Mad Men. *Don Draper, the lead character in the series, enjoyed this cocktail in several episodes.*

*Although many people treat the Old Fashioned as a built drink to be constructed in its final serving glass, I side with leading bartenders Jeffery Morgenthaler, Julie Reiner, and Jim Meehan, who all recommend that it be stirred with ice in a mixing glass, then poured over fresh ice in a chilled old fashioned glass. Made this way, it is properly chilled and diluted at the very first sip.*

*The classic recipe, which evolved over two centuries ago, calls for just three ingredients: whiskey, a sugar cube or sugar syrup, and a dash or two of Angostura Bitters. During Prohibition, a second version became popular, featuring cherries and a slice of orange muddled in the bottom of the glass. The latter version can be a refreshing and pleasant drink, particularly for novice whiskey drinkers. But I prefer to focus on the original 200-year-old recipe, with three syrup options to sweeten the cocktail.*

| 2 ounces | *Elijah Craig Small Batch Bourbon or George Dickel Rye* |
| 1–1½ teaspoons | *simple syrup (for the classic recipe) or demerara simple syrup or vanilla-infused demerara syrup (see Chapter 7: Custom-Made Cocktail Syrups for recipes for the above three syrups)* |
| 2 dashes | *Angostura Bitters (2 dashes equals ¼ teaspoon)* |

## Recipe

1. Combine the ingredients in a chilled mixing glass, including one teaspoon of the syrup of your choice. Add ice cubes and stir for about 30 seconds until cold.

2. Taste the drink and if it is not as smooth as you would like, consider adding a little more syrup. Or simply stir the drink a little longer, allowing the melting ice to dilute it further, which will also smooth it out.

3. Strain into a chilled old fashioned glass.

4. If you are using bourbon, cut a five-inch strip of orange peel with a channel knife, allowing the orange zest oil to spray onto the surface of the cocktail. If you are using rye whiskey, simply substitute a lemon peel for the orange peel.

5. Twist the citrus strip into a corkscrew around the handle of your barspoon and slide it off the end. You now have a proverbial citrus twist.

6. Hang one end over the rim of the glass as a visual garnish. Let the other end drift into the cocktail where it will add a little more flavor to the drink.

7. Finally, add fresh ice, preferably large cubes that will keep the drink cold while not diluting it much further.

8. Consider adding a Tillen Farms Merry Maraschino Cherry as an additional garnish.

## Recipe Notes

You can use regular simple syrup, demerara simple syrup, or vanilla-infused demerara syrup in this recipe. I personally think the vanilla-infused demerara syrup takes this cocktail, particularly when it is made with bourbon, to a whole new level.

The recent innovation of aging maple syrup in oak barrels formerly used to age bourbon whiskey provides an entirely new option for sweetening Bourbon Old Fashioneds. Roughly a dozen brands of bourbon-barrel-aged maple syrup are on the market today, any of which can be substituted for the syrups mentioned above. I've tried two: Pappy Van Winkle Bourbon Barrel-Aged Pure Maple Syrup is my favorite, but BLiS is also very good. When using maple syrup to sweeten an Old Fashioned, start with just one teaspoon per cocktail.

Many older recipes for this drink call for muddling the bitters with a sugar cube and a small amount of water. But I agree with David Embury that using some form of sugar syrup is simpler, and syrup ensures that the cocktail will have the same level of sweetness from the first sip to the last.

## History

Most cocktail histories credit the Pendennis Club in Louisville, Kentucky, for developing the Old Fashioned—their source being a 1931 book titled *Old Waldorf Bar Days*, by Albert Stevens Crockett. However, the cocktail writer Robert Simonson does a skillful job of repudiating that claim. In his recent book, *The Old-Fashioned*, Simonson points out that Jacques Straub, who managed the Pendennis Club for 20 years, published a cocktail book in 1914 simply titled *Drinks*. Straub included a recipe for the Old Fashioned in that book without making any reference to the drink's having been created at his club. Simonson argues that if the Old Fashioned had originated there, Straub certainly would have claimed it.

As mentioned in Chapter 1, a New York newspaper in 1806 defined the cocktail as "a stimulating liquor composed of spirits of any kind, sugar, water, and bitters." If you selected whiskey as the spirit in the above recipe, you would be making a whiskey Old Fashioned.

The drink, sometimes known as a Whiskey Cocktail, was a favorite among Union Army generals during the Civil War. Legend has it that after the war, bartenders began to add various liqueurs to the drink. Drinkers rebelled and began asking for "an old-fashioned Whiskey Cocktail," a request that eventually became "an Old Fashioned."

*The official
cocktail of
New Orleans*

# SAZERAC

*This cocktail, with both a terrific name and a very color-ful history, is one of the few cocktails that incorporates absinthe, once banned for its supposed hallucinatory properties.*

| | |
|---|---|
| **2 ounces** | **rye whiskey** *(see recipe notes below)* |
| **1½ teaspoons** | **simple syrup** *(see Chapter 7: Custom-Made Cocktail Syrups)* |
| **1 dash** | **Angostura Bitters** |
| **3 dashes** | **Peychaud Bitters** |
| **1 dash** | **Absente Absinthe** |

## *Recipe*

1. Combine all ingredients in a chilled mixing glass. Add ice cubes and stir until cold.

2. Srain into a chilled old fashioned glass *without* ice.

3. Cut a five-inch strip of lemon peel with a channel knife, allowing the zest oil to spray onto the surface of the cocktail.

4. Twist the strip into a corkscrew around the handle of your barspoon and slide it off the end. You now have the proverbial citrus twist.

5. Drop the twist into the cocktail where it will add a little more flavor to the drink.

## Recipe Notes

Many cocktail writers believe the Sazerac tastes better when it's not too chilled. But if you prefer to have this cocktail on the rocks, that's a fine option, too. Simply add fresh ice cubes to the finished drink.

Cognac was the base spirit for the Sazerac until the 1870s, when a phylloxera epidemic destroyed many of the cognac vineyards in France. Out of desperation, bartenders shifted to rye in their Sazeracs, and rye has been the base spirit of this cocktail ever since.

Crown Royal Northern Harvest Rye makes a fine Sazerac. But Sazerac Rye, as you might assume, also works well in this drink.

## History

Antoine Peychaud was the son of wealthy coffee plantation owners who fled Haiti for New Orleans as a result of the Haitian slave revolt of 1804. As a young man, he trained as an apothecary, creating and selling herbal remedies to the citizens of New Orleans. These remedies—various mixtures of plants and alcohol—were known as "bitters," obviously because of their taste.

In 1830, Antoine modified a family recipe to create what became known as Peychaud's Bitters. Roughly 10 years later, he began combining these bitters with the French cognac Sazerac-de-Forge-et-Fils, offering the mixture in a small egg cup known as a *coquetier*. He called the drink a Sazerac.

New Orleanians have since jumped to the conclusion that the French word *coquetier* is surely a precursor to the English word *cocktail*—and that the Sazerac must therefore be the country's first cocktail. But while many good things come from New Orleans, America's first cocktail is probably not one of them. We know this because the word *cocktail* first appeared in 1806 in the New York newspaper *The Balance and Columbian Repository*—roughly 34 years before Antoine Peychaud created his Sazerac.

The popularity of the Sazerac spread quickly, not only in the bars of New Orleans, but also in the coffeehouses where, unlike in bars, women were permitted to drink.

## Cocktail Tip:

*A cocktail should always taste better than any of its individual ingredients.*

As Jeff Hollinger and Rob Schwartz point out in *Art of the Bar,* a cocktail should taste better than any of its individual ingredients. I find both freshly squeezed orange juice and good champagne delicious. In my opinion, you are far better off enjoying each separately, rather than combining them in a Mimosa. ❧

*Popularized as a
pre-dinner cocktail by
Reginald Vanderbilt*

# STINGER

*The Stinger is a classic cocktail with a history that includes both New York high society in the 1920s and '30s, and fighter pilots in World War II. When made with quality ingredients, it can be excellent.*

| | |
|---|---|
| *2 ounces* | **Remy Martin VSOP Cognac** |
| *2 teaspoons* | **Tempus Fugit Crème de Menthe Glaciale** |

## Recipe

1. Combine the ingredients in a chilled mixing glass. Add ice cubes and stir until cold.

2. Strain into a chilled old fashioned glass over finely cracked or crushed ice.

3. Garnish with a couple of sprigs of fresh spearmint that you've slapped against the back of your hand to release their aroma.

## Recipe Notes

Finding top-quality white crème de menthe for this cocktail can be challenging. Most brands on the market taste pretty bad. However, several cocktail writers are now recommending the relatively new Tempus Fugit Crème de Menthe Glaciale.

Most Stinger recipes call for shaking this cocktail to chill it. But one of the basic rules of bartending is that unless a cocktail contains citrus, egg white, or dairy, it should be stirred—*not* shaken. Moreover, the cracked or crushed ice in the finished cocktail will ensure that it's every bit as cold as a shaken cocktail.

## History

Since cognac is the base liquor in the Stinger, it was first served as an after-dinner drink among New York's elite in the 1890s. According to cocktail historian David Wondrich, Reginald Vanderbilt loved the drink so much that he changed that tradition in the 1920s by routinely ordering Stingers before dinner at New York's popular Colony Restaurant. His high-society friends quickly followed suit.

The drink continued its popularity throughout World War II. During that time, American fighter pilots were known to celebrate successful combat missions by ordering a round of Stingers.

# CHAPTER 5

# SHAKEN

# SHAKEN COCKTAILS

*A shaken cocktail is one that's chilled and diluted by shaking ingredients together with ice in a cocktail shaker.*

Shaken cocktails tend to be colder because shaking is much more efficient at chilling than stirring. And because they are more diluted and much more aerated than a stirred cocktail, they also tend to be smoother and more mellow, which makes them easier for novice drinkers to enjoy.

Still, shaken cocktails are somewhat harder to master than stirred cocktails because of the challenge of learning to work effectively with a shaker.

## Recommendations for making better shaken cocktails:

- Get yourself an all-metal Boston shaker. While glass-and-metal shakers are common in the marketplace, a Boston shaker that consists of two metal parts is the shaker of choice for experienced bartenders. Why? As New York cocktail writer and bartender Toby Cecchini points out, all-metal shakers fit together more tightly than glass-and-metal varieties. Moreover, they produce a colder finished cocktail. (*Note:* Bartenders refer to the metal parts of a Boston shaker as *tins*, even though they're made of stainless steel.)

- Always prechill your cocktail glasses in the freezer for 15 minutes or more. This will help ensure that your finished cocktail stays chilled longer.

- If a cocktail incorporates a carbonated liquid such as club soda or sparkling wine, do not add that carbonated liquid until *after* the cocktail has been shaken. Otherwise the carbonation will be lost during the shaking process.

- Build the drink in the smaller of the two tins, and add ice to a level one inch below the rim of the tin.

## Techniques for using cocktail shakers

1. Fill the smaller of the two shaking tins with ingredients and ice and place it on the bar. Fit the larger tin over the mouth of the smaller one, with the base of the larger tin pointing slightly off vertical. One writer explains this best by saying the larger tin should be angled so the two tins resemble the

curve of a banana. This will make the tins easier to separate once the shaking is completed.

2.   Holding the small tin with one hand, hit the flat base of the large tin (the part closest to the ceiling) smartly with the palm of your other hand. You want to hit it just hard enough to form a seal, but not so hard that it will be difficult to separate the tins after the cocktail is shaken. This is an art that only comes with practice.

3.   Test the seal between the two shakers by lifting the large tin a quarter of an inch off the bar. If the seal between the two tins is sufficient, the small tin will remain attached to the large one. If the small tin breaks away, simply repeat steps 1 and 2 and test again for a good seal.

4.   Once the two tins have a good seal, reverse their position so that the smaller tin is on top. Assuming you are right-handed, grab the bottom of the large tin tightly with the thumb and middle finger of your left hand, and the bottom of the small tin with the thumb and middle finger of your right hand. By using just the thumb and middle finger of each hand, you minimize the transfer of heat from your hands to the cocktail.

5.   Raise the shaker just above your shoulder and position it so the two tins are roughly horizontal to the floor.

6.   Vigorously propel the shaker forward and backward horizontally to complete one (roundtrip) shake. You should hear the ice crash against the end of the tins each time you reverse direction. Continue shaking until you have completed 36 (roundtrip) shakes in roughly 12 seconds.

7.   Place the base of the large tin on the bar. Turn the base so that the small tin is pointing at the 3 o'clock position. Tightly squeeze the large tin with your thumb and middle finger at the 6 and 12 o'clock positions, then straighten the small tin into a vertical position with your other hand. If you apply enough pressure at the 6 and 12 o'clock positions, the partial vacuum generated by the chilled cocktail will vent and the two tins will come apart. (Some wiggling back and forth usually helps.) This technique works 99 percent of the time.

Obviously, the key to success lies in having hit the large tin just hard enough in step 2 to achieve a seal that prevents leaks—but not so hard that the seal between the two tins is difficult to break. With practice, you will learn exactly how to do this. Mastering this skill is one of the measures of a good bartender.

8. If the two tins fail to separate, go to Plan B: rotate the tins so the small tin is bent toward the 6 o'clock position. Grasp the large tin firmly with the palm of your left hand, and hit its rim at the 3 o'clock position with the heel of your right hand. The small tin generally breaks free after one or two blows to the rim of the large tin.

9. Pour the cocktail and ice from the large tin into the small tin. Place a Hawthorne strainer over the small tin, and while holding the strainer in place with your index finger, strain the cocktail into a chilled cocktail glass (see illustration at right). The Hawthorne strainer is much less likely to slip out of your grasp when used with the smaller tin.

10. *Note:* The Hawthorne strainer allows you to adjust the opening between the strainer's plate and the rim of the tin. To close the opening, you simply push the tab that sticks out of the plate with your index finger. This action, known in the industry as "closing the gate," filters out particles of citrus pulp and small pieces of ice that would otherwise make it into the glass. While the positioning of the gate is a matter of personal taste, some cocktail writers argue that filtering out shards of ice is a good idea since they would otherwise melt and too quickly dilute the cocktail.

*A superb variation on a standard Daiquiri*

# CONSTANTE'S DAIQUIRI #3

*This daiquiri was created by Constantino Rib-alaigua Vert at La Floridita, the bar he owned in Havana, Cuba, from 1918 to 1952. Constantino, who went by the nickname "Constante," had a special interest in the Daiquiri, creating five variations in all. Of those, Daiquiri #3 is considered his best.*

*Constante's Daiquiri #3 includes two ingredients not found in regular daiquiris: maraschino liqueur, and freshly squeezed grapefruit juice. The resulting cocktail is surprisingly complex and nuanced.*

| | |
|---|---|
| *1 ounce* | **Mount Gay Eclipse Rum** |
| *1 ounce* | **Mount Gay Silver Eclipse Rum** |
| *1 ounce* | **freshly squeezed lime juice** |
| *½ ounce* | **simple syrup** (see Chapter 7: Custom-Made Cocktail Syrups) |
| *¾ ounce* | **freshly squeezed grapefruit juice** |
| *1 teaspoon* | **Luxardo Maraschino Liqueur** |

## Recipe

1. Combine the ingredients in a cocktail shaker. Add ice cubes and shake until cold.
2. Strain into a chilled martini glass.
3. Garnish with a wedge of grapefruit or a half-wheel of lime.
4. Consider adding as a third garnish a sprig of fresh mint that you have slapped against the back of your hand to release its aroma.

## Recipe Notes

Constante alternated between preparing this cocktail by shaking it with ice cubes and chilling it with ice in a blender (the classic "frozen daiquiri"). In my opinion, the former is the better drink.

Most writers suggest using either white rum or light rum for this cocktail. However, the combination of two Mount Gay Rums adds greater complexity to the drink.

Many recipes call for an abundance of maraschino liqueur to offset the acidity of the citrus juices. But the perfume taste of maraschino can easily overpower the drink. This recipe dials down the maraschino and offsets the acidity of the citrus with simple syrup instead. The amount of simple syrup you use will depend on the sweetness of the two citrus juices you squeeze on a particular day. As always, taste the cocktail and add more simple syrup if necessary.

# History

Constante, who had worked in bars since the age of 16, became known as *El Rey de los Coteleros,* or *King of the Cocktails*. According to writer David Embury, Constante avoided using citrus presses to squeeze fresh lime juice, because he worried that a press might also extract bitterness from the lime's pith. Instead, he used only his fingers to extract the juice. By the end of his career, Constante estimated he had hand-squeezed over 80 million limes.

Ernest Hemingway, who moved to Havana in 1939 to spend more time writing, noticed Constante making Daiquiris at La Floridita one day and asked to taste what appears to have been a Daiquiri #3. Since he was concerned about diabetes, he asked Constante to modify the Daiquiri #3 by reducing the sugar and doubling the amount of rum. Hemingway's modified version lives on to this day, going by the name *Papa Doble*—"*Papa*" being Hemingway's nickname, and "*Doble*" referring to the double ration of rum. Hemingway became a regular at La Floridita, sitting at the end of the bar for hours, reading and sipping *Papa Dobles*. One day, he reputedly finished 17 *Papa Dobles* before leaving the bar.

Constante died in 1952, but La Floridita bar is still in business today with a life-size bronze statue of Hemingway sitting at his regular seat at the bar.

On a personal note, when I was 15, my father decided to take our family to Havana, despite U.S. State Department warnings that Castro had just taken over Cuba. Pop took us to *jai alai* matches and to many of the bars and restaurants that Hemingway frequented. One of them was La Floridita—among the many places I visited in my teens and twenties, only to learn later in life how special they really were.

At one moment in La Floridita, my mother realized that my seven-year-old brother, Terry, had wandered away from the bar. A patron in the bar, noticing her distress, offered to help. He organized a search party, and a large portion of the bar's customers made their way into the street to find my errant brother. The posse quickly apprehended him, and my father showed his appreciation by buying a round for the house.

*An unforgettable drink
with a curious name*

# CORPSE REVIVER #2

*The Corpse Reviver #2 gets great reviews from cocktail writers for good reason. Moreover, its offbeat name and the suffix #2 add to its mystique. Order a Corpse Reviver #2 in any bar and heads will turn.*

| | |
|---|---|
| ¾ ounce | **Tanqueray Gin** |
| ¾ ounce | **Cointreau** |
| ¾ ounce | **Cocchi Americano aperitif wine** |
| ½ ounce | **lemon juice** |
| 1–2 dashes | **Absente Absinthe** |

## Recipe

1. Combine all ingredients in a cocktail shaker. Add ice cubes and shake until cold.

2. Strain into a chilled martini glass.

3. Cut a six-inch strip of lemon peel with a channel knife, allowing the zest oil to spray onto the surface of this cocktail.

4. Twist the strip into a corkscrew around the handle of your barspoon and slide it off the end. You now have a proverbial citrus twist.

5. Hang one end of the twist over the rim of the glass as a visual garnish. Let the other end drift into the cocktail where it will add a little more flavor to the drink.

6. Consider adding a Tillen Farms Merry Maraschino Cherry as an additional garnish.

## Recipe Notes

In his *Savoy Cocktail Book,* Harry Craddock calls for equal parts gin, Cointreau, Kina Lillet, and lemon juice. But I find that using an equal part of lemon juice results in a fairly tart cocktail, which is not to my taste. In this recipe, I've dialed back the lemon juice to ½ ounce. Then I use lemon zest oil to greatly enhance the taste of this drink

Kina Lillet is no longer available. In 1985, the Lillet company changed the formulation of the aperitif, making it slightly milder and renaming it Lillet Blanc. Some bartenders bemoan that change and recommend using Cocchi Americano aperitif wine instead, which they claim has a flavor closer to the original Kina Lillet. I have used both Lillet Blanc and Cocchi Americano and find that I have a definite preference for the latter in this cocktail. (You can find Cocchi Americano aperitif wine in better liquor stores.)

## History

The first recipe for the Corpse Reviver appeared in the 1871 book *Gentleman's Table Guide.* Some 60 years later, Harry Craddock listed two versions of the cocktail—Corpse Revivers #1 and #2—in his *Savoy Cocktail Book.* The Corpse Reviver #2 is considered the better of the pair.

As often happens with classic cocktails, the Corpse Reviver #2 was all but forgotten by the middle of the last century. It was Ted Haigh who resurrected it in 2009 in his excellent *Vintage Spirits and Forgotten Cocktails:* he lavished more praise on this one drink than on any other cocktail in his book. One sip, and you will understand why.

In the early lexicon of cocktails, the term *Reviver* referred to a drink that would help you wake up and get going in the morning. Craddock confirmed this theory with a comment under his Corpse Reviver #1 recipe: "To be taken before 11 a.m., or whenever steam and energy are needed." He did add a warning to his own Corpse Reviver #2 recipe: "Four of these taken in swift succession will un-revive the corpse again." While a cup of coffee may be a better strategy for getting started in the morning, the Corpse Reviver #2 is an elegant way to begin an evening.

*A favorite of Carrie Bradshaw in Sex and the City*

# COSMOPOLITAN

*The Cosmopolitan is a gentle, light-flavored cocktail, which explains its popularity among novice drinkers.*

*Some people might question why I'm including a cocktail invented in the 1980s in a book that features classic cocktails. I believe the Cosmopolitan deserves recognition because it was one of the key drinks that led the way out of the cocktail doldrums of the 1970s and into the cocktail renaissance of the late '80s. Jeff Hollinger and Rob Schwartz, in their book* The Art of the Bar, *agree that the Cosmopolitan qualifies as a classic cocktail.*

| | |
|---|---|
| *2 ounces* | *Absolut Citron Vodka* |
| *1 ounce* | *Cointreau* |
| *1 tablespoon* | *freshly squeezed lime juice* |
| *1 ounce* | *Ocean Spray Cranberry Juice (not Cranberry Juice Cocktail)* |
| *¾ teaspoon* | *Grand Marnier* |

## *Recipe*

1. Combine the ingredients in a cocktail shaker. Add ice cubes and shake until cold.
2. Strain into a chilled martini glass.
3. Garnish with a wheel of lime, sliced to perch on the rim of the glass.

## Recipe Notes

This recipe uses several strategies to give this traditionally gentle cocktail a little more character. First, it calls for slightly more vodka and Cointreau. Also, it backs up the Cointreau with ¾ teaspoon of its stronger cousin Grand Marnier. And finally, it calls for cranberry **juice** rather than cranberry juice cocktail. Try one made this way, and I predict you'll never go back.

## History

Some writers attribute this cocktail to famed bartender Dale Degroff, but Degroff has waved off any credit. Neal Murray, a Minneapolis bartender, made a prototype Cosmopolitan in 1975 when he added cranberry juice to a Kamikase, a cocktail made with vodka, triple sec, and lime juice. Unfortunately, Murray's creation did not catch on, and he became a footnote in the drink's history.

Thanks to Gary Regan, a renowned cocktail writer, the person who should get the most credit for creating this cocktail is Miami bartender Cheryl Cooke. In the mid-1980s she observed that many of her customers ordered Martinis simply to be seen with that elegant glass in hand, but clearly didn't enjoy the taste of the drink itself. She decided to create an entirely new drink—one that combined Absolut Citron, triple sec, cranberry juice, and Rose's Lime Juice—and chose to serve it in a martini glass. The new cocktail was an immediate success.

New York bartenders Melissa Huffsmith and Toby Checchini deserve credit for improving Cooke's creation. They upgraded the triple sec to Cointreau and replaced the repugnant Rose's Lime Juice with freshly squeezed juice.

The cocktail's popularity rose when Madonna was photographed drinking a "Cosmo" at a Grammy Awards party in 1988 held in Dale Degroff's bar at the Rainbow Room on the 65th floor of New York's Rockefeller Center. But probably the biggest factor in the Cosmopolitan's success was when the lead characters in HBO's 1998 series *Sex in the City* adopted the Cosmo as their drink of choice.

The essence of
the Caribbean

# DAIQUIRI

*The Daiquiri is another of the six basic cocktails that writer David Embury felt every home bartender should learn to make. Embury believed the Daiquiri deserved to be even more popular than it was when he wrote his classic book* The Fine Art of Mixing Drinks *in 1948. He claimed it ranked above the Manhattan in overall quality. President Kennedy and his wife, Jackie, must have agreed, because the Daiquiri was their favorite cocktail. Unfortunately, in the spirit of convenience that ruled the 1950s and early '60s, they used frozen limeade in their Daiquiris.*

| | |
|---|---|
| *2 ounces* | ***El Dorado 3-Year Cask-Aged Demerara Rum from Guyana*** |
| *1 ounce* | ***freshly squeezed lime juice*** |
| *¾ ounce* | ***simple syrup*** *(see Chapter 7: Custom-Made Cocktail Syrups)* |

## Recipe

1. Combine the ingredients in a cocktail shaker. Add ice cubes and shake until cold.
2. Strain into a chilled martini glass.
3. Garnish with a half-slice of lime over the rim of the glass.

## Recipe Notes

El Dorado 3-Year Cask-Aged Rum makes a delicious and nuanced Daiquiri.

Note that leading cocktail writers and bartenders have slightly varying opinions as to the proper ratio of rum, lime juice, and simple syrup to make the perfect Daiquiri. If the recipe above seems too sweet or too tart, simply adjust the cocktail to your taste by adding more lime juice or simple syrup.

The above recipe is *not* a frozen Daiquiri. In the 1970s and '80s, both the Margarita and the Daiquiri fell on hard times, as they degenerated into "frozen" drinks, often dispensed from machines that resembled soft-serve ice cream dispensers. It was a low point for both cocktails. Although frozen Daiquiris still have their fans, a traditional Daiquiri served straight up in a chilled martini glass is a sophisticated cocktail—and the best representation of what a Daiquiri can be.

## History

While the first Daiquiri was mixed on the island of Cuba, two Americans get credit for its creation and subsequent popularity.

On June 22, 1898, during the Spanish-American War, U.S. naval ships opened fire on a Cuban village named Daiquiri prior to landing an invasion force. The village was destroyed, and a 16,000-man army, which included Teddy Roosevelt and his Rough Riders, waded ashore. The Spanish surrendered 25 days later near the city of Santiago.

The mountains around Daiquiri were rich with iron ore, and American mining companies soon took over several mines. Jennings Cox, an American mining engineer, arrived to run a mine known as the "Daiquiri Mine." According to his granddaughter, Cox was entertaining guests one evening when he ran out of gin. With guests clamoring for drinks, Cox reached for a bottle of local rum, combined it with lime juice and sugar, and created an entirely new cocktail. One of the guests, named Pagliuchi, proposed that the new drink be named after the mine.

Several years later, the USS *Minnesota* anchored in nearby Guantanamo Bay, and the ship's medical officer, Lucius Johnson, went ashore to explore Spanish-American war sites. Johnson visited both the invasion beach and the nearby Daiquiri mine, where he ran into Jennings Cox, who proceeded to offer him a Daiquiri. According to Wayne Curtis's excellent book *And a Bottle of Rum,* Johnson was so impressed with the cocktail that he took the recipe back to the Army-Navy Club in Washington, DC. The drink was well received, and the club bar was soon renamed the Daiquiri Lounge. Johnson went on to be named a rear admiral, and the Daiquiri became one of the most popular cocktails in the nation. Cox's fate is unknown, but he deserves recognition as the creator of this excellent drink.

*Elegant and smooth,
but packs a punch*

# CFRENCH 75

*The French 75 cocktail got its name from a French artillery piece widely adopted by the Allies in World War I. The powerful gun had a reputation for operating smoothly among the servicemen of that war. Harry Craddock commented, in his* Savoy Cocktail Book, *that the French 75 cocktail, like the artillery piece, "hits with remarkable precision."*

*Harry Truman, who commanded a French 75 gunnery unit in France during World War I, commented from the battlefield, "I'd rather be here than be president of the United States." I'm sure there were many times after he became president that he felt the same way.*

| | |
|---|---|
| *1¼ ounces* | *Tanqueray Gin* |
| *½ ounce* | *simple syrup (see Chapter 7: Custom-Made Cocktail Syrups)* |
| *½ ounce* | *lemon juice* |
| *3 ounces* | *chilled sparkling wine (see recipe notes below)* |

## Recipe

1. Combine all the ingredients, except the sparkling wine, in a cocktail shaker. Add ice cubes and shake until cold.

2. Strain into a chilled champagne flute filled with the chilled sparkling wine.

3. Cut a six-inch strip of lemon peel with a channel knife. Twist the strip into a corkscrew around the handle of your barspoon and slide it off the end. You now have a proverbial citrus twist.

4. Hang one end over the rim of the flute as a visual garnish.

## Recipe Notes

Depending on the tartness of the lemon juice and the dryness of your sparkling wine, you may need to adjust the ratio of simple syrup and lemon juice in the above recipe.

I've used Zonin Brut Prosecco, Korbel Sonoma Brut Champagne, and Gloria Ferrer Sonoma Brut Champagne. They all made excellent French 75s. But the Zonin is an especially good value.

Some bartenders add strawberries or other fruit to make a French 75 more festive.

## History

Recipes for the French 75 started appearing in cocktail books after World War I, including Harry MacElhone's *Harry's ABC of Mixing Cocktails*, and Harry Craddock's *Savoy Cocktail Book*. The base spirit used in these recipes is usually either cognac or gin. It is said that American pilots of the Lafayette Escadrille, upon returning from combat missions during the First World War, toasted each other with a French 75 made with cognac. I've tried both versions and prefer the one made with gin.

## Cocktail Tip:

*When making a cocktail in a shaker or mixing glass, add the ice last.*

The reason is simple: if you have to stop making the cocktail to search for a missing ingredient or to answer the door, the ice is not diluting your partially made drink. 🍸

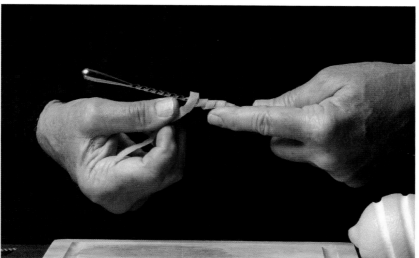

*First enjoyed by officers on British warships*

# GIMLET

*In Raymond Chandler's 1953 novel* The Long Goodbye, *Terry Lennox makes the following observation: "A real Gimlet is half gin and half Rose's lime juice and nothing else. It beats Martinis hollow."*

*A well-made Gimlet can indeed go down better than an average Martini. But the traditional recipe for a Gimlet—the one that calls for Rose's Sweetened Lime Juice—has its drawbacks. Rose's is made from lime juice concentrate sweetened with high-fructose corn syrup, is preserved with sodium metabisulfite, and is colored with blue dye #1—and in my opinion, it has a distinctly artificial taste.*

*Instead, I recommend substituting lime cordial (see the recipe on next page) for Rose's Sweetened Lime Juice. To add a twist to the character Terry Lennox's quotation, a Gimlet made with lime cordial beats hollow one made with Rose's Sweetened Lime Juice.*

| | |
|---|---|
| *2 ounces* | **Plymouth Gin** |
| *1 ounce* | **lime cordial** *(see recipe on page 118)* |

## Recipe

1. Combine the ingredients in a cocktail shaker. Add ice cubes and shake until cold.

2. Strain into a chilled martini glass.

3. Garnish with a wedge of lime perched on the rim.

## Recipe for
## Lime Cordial

| | |
|---|---|
| ½ teaspoon | freshly grated lime zest |
| ½ ounce | simple syrup (see Chapter 7: Custom-Made Cocktail Syrups) |
| ½ ounce | freshly squeezed lime juice |

Use a Microplane or similar zester to grate the lime zest. Try to scrape off only the green peel, as too much of the white pith can make the drink bitter. Marinate the zest in the simple syrup for 10 minutes. Strain out the zest and add ½ ounce of freshly squeezed lime juice to the syrup. 🎩

## Recipe Notes

This cocktail lends itself well to superchilling in the freezer for roughly 15 minutes to reduce the temperature to approximately 19°F.

## History

Until the middle of the eighteenth century, the British Navy struggled with scurvy, a disease caused by long periods at sea without access to vitamin C. Often during wartime, more sailors died from scurvy than were killed in combat.

In 1753 a Scottish physician named James Lind proposed that citrus juice would prevent the disease. In 1795 the British Navy began adding lemon, and later lime, juice to enlisted sailors' daily rum rations, after which scurvy stopped being a problem. As a result of this practice, British sailors were often referred to as *limeys*.

While the British Navy's enlisted men enjoyed daily rum rations, British naval officers traditionally drank gin—specifically, Plymouth Gin. Thus, the first Gimlet cocktail was probably created on a British warship in the "officers wardroom" (the naval term for the officers' dining compartment) when they added lime juice to their gin for protection from scurvy.

Unfortunately, fresh limes would begin to spoil a week or two into a voyage. The navy responded by juicing limes and adding rum to the juice as a preservative. From that tradition, a Scotsman named Lauchlan Rose developed in 1867 an alcohol-free product known as Rose's Lime Cordial, which became Rose's Sweetened Lime Juice in the United States.

Two theories arose as to how the Gimlet got its name. The most popular one suggests that the cocktail was named for Rear Admiral Thomas Gimlette, Surgeon General of the British Navy, who in the late 1800s recommended the addition of lime juice to officers' gin to prevent scurvy. But this theory is doubtful, since by the time he made this recommendation, the British Navy had been adding lime juice to enlisted sailors' rum rations for roughly a hundred years. Are we to believe officers waited so long to protect themselves? Not likely.

A second, much more believable, theory posits that the cocktail was named for a corkscrew tool called a *gimlet* that sailors used to opened lime juice containers in the 1800s. The names for the tool and the cocktail are spelled the same, something that is not true for Rear Admiral Gimlette's name.

*Particularly good
with custom-
made orgeat
syrup*

# MAI TAI

*In 1944, two friends from Tahiti came to visit Victor Bergeron, a.k.a. Trader Vic, at his bar in Oakland, California. Bergeron served them a cocktail that combined J. Wray & Nephew 17-Year-Old Rum, orange Curaçao, lime juice, simple syrup, and orgeat syrup. His friends took one sip and exclaimed "Mai tai, roa ae!" which is Tahitian for "Out of this world! The best!" Their enthusiastic praise led to the name of the new cocktail.*

*As time passed, the Mai Tai fell on hard times when bartenders began using economy rums and bottled cocktail mixes. But when it's made with quality ingredients, particularly custom-made orgeat syrup, the Mai Tai absolutely lives up to its Polynesian name.*

| | |
|---|---|
| *2 ounces* | ***El Dorado 8-Year-Old Demerara Rum*** |
| *4 teaspoons* | ***Pierre Ferrand Dry Orange Curaçao*** |
| *1 ounce* | ***freshly squeezed lime juice*** |
| *¾ ounce* | ***custom-made orgeat syrup*** <br> *(see Chapter 7: Custom-Made Cocktail Syrups)* |

## Recipe

1. Combine the ingredients in a cocktail shaker. Add ice cubes and shake until cold.

2. Pour into an old fashioned glass filled with crushed ice.

3. As a garnish, insert one or two halves of the limes you squeezed for juice into the crushed ice.

4. For an additional garnish, take a few sprigs of spearmint you've slapped against the back of your hand to release their aroma, and stick them into the crushed ice near the rim of the glass.

## Recipe Notes

When I discovered that J. Wray & Nephew 17-Year-Old Rum was no longer available, I researched rums recommended by no fewer than 11 top cocktail writers. There was hardly any consensus. After much trial and error, I found that El Dorado 8-Year Demerara Rum is a good choice for this cocktail. But if you cannot get that variety of rum, I recommend combining one ounce of Mount Gay Black Barrel Rum with one ounce of Mount Gay Eclipse Rum.

For the orange liqueur, most recipes call for orange Curaçao. Pierre Ferrand Dry Curaçao, which was developed in cooperation with cocktail writer David Wondrich, is an excellent choice for this drink. Start with four teaspoons and taste for balance. If the drink is slightly tart, add another teaspoon.

Orgeat, an almond-flavored syrup, is literally the defining element of this cocktail. Moreover, making your own orgeat syrup is the key to a world-class Mai Tai. If that is not an option, a decent alternative is Small Hand Foods Orgeat Syrup, made by an artisanal California company that specializes in producing pre-Prohibition cocktail ingredients.

## History

Another bartender also claims credit for the Mai Tai. In 1933, Ernest Raymond Beaumont Gantt, a.k.a. Don the Beachcomber, created a drink that he, too, called the Mai Tai. Gantt's Mai Tai differs from Bergeron's by incorporating falernum, Pernod, grapefruit juice, and Angostura Bitters. Although Gantt created his drink 11 years earlier than Bergeron, most current Mai Tai recipes have more in common with Bergeron's version.

Bergeron and Gantt ran competing Polynesian restaurant chains that became particularly popular after World War II as veterans returned from the Pacific island campaigns.

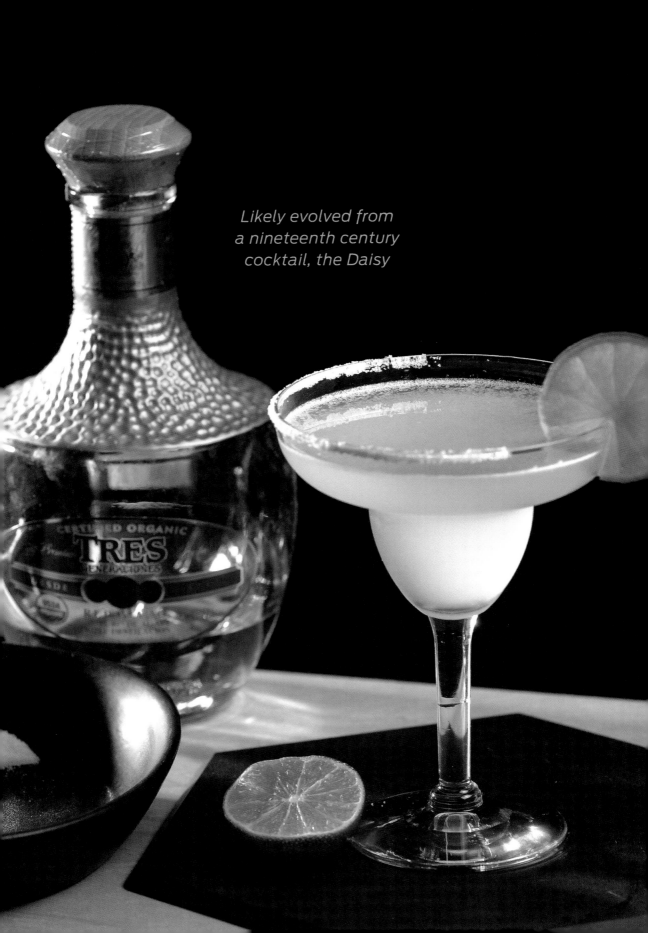

*Likely evolved from a nineteenth century cocktail, the Daisy*

# MARGARITA

*The Margarita has become one of the most popular cocktails in the country. When made properly with quality ingredients, it can also be an excellent drink. The recipe below differs from most in two ways. First, it incorporates lime zest oil to add complexity to the drink. Second, it uses one of the more mellow tequilas on the market— Tres Generaciones Reposado. These two ingredients combine with the Cointreau to make a subtle, more-nuanced Margarita than you will get in most bars.*

| | |
|---|---|
| 1½ ounces | **Tres Generaciones Reposado Tequila** *(see recipe notes)* |
| 1 ounce | **Cointreau** |
| ½ ounce | **freshly squeezed lime juice** |
| ½ teaspoon | **freshly grated lime zest** *(see recipe notes)* |
| ¼ ounce | **simple syrup** *(see Chapter 7: Custom-Made Cocktail Syrups)* |

## Recipe

1. Wash one lime.

2. Using a Microplane zester or box grater, grate the lime, scraping off only the green layer of the skin and avoiding the white pith.

3. Add the grated zest to the lime juice and let the mixture marinate for five minutes.

4. Strain out the grated lime zest and combine the juice with the tequila, Cointreau, and simple syrup in a cocktail shaker.

5. Add ice cubes and shake until cold.

6. Strain the finished drink into a chilled Margarita glass and garnish with a slice of lime perched on the rim.

## Recipe Notes

Tequilas come in three basic categories, based on the amount of time they have been aged. Silver or Blanco tequilas are aged up to two months. Reposado tequilas are aged from two months to one year. Any tequila aged over one year is an Anejo, and generally reserved for sipping straight, instead of blending in cocktails.

Many Margarita recipes call for Silver or Blanco Tequila, but Reposado tequilas possess more character and smoothness—and those characteristics can greatly enhance this drink. Tres Generaciones Reposado is a particularly smooth, triple-distilled, organic Tequila. If you cannot find Tres Generaciones, both Partida Reposado and Espolon Reposado are good alternatives.

*America's Test Kitchen,* the TV program that has proposed many new approaches to cooking, gets credit for the idea of marinating lime zest in lime juice when making a Margarita. The hosts actually suggest mixing lemons *and* limes in this drink. I prefer using lime zest and juice only, as limes are more traditional in a Margarita.

*Note:* The above recipe doesn't mention salting the rim of the glass. If you like the idea of a traditional salted rim, some cocktail writers suggest salting just half the rim, so your guests have the option of sipping the cocktail with or without the salt.

To be clear, the above recipe does *not* produce a "frozen" Margarita. In the 1970s and '80s, both the Margarita and the Daiquiri fell on, shall we say, hard times, degenerating into "frozen" drinks that were often dispensed from machines that resembled soft-serve ice cream dispensers. Although frozen Margaritas still have their fans, a traditional Margarita is served straight up in a chilled Margarita glass.

## History

For decades, bartenders on both sides of our Southern border have claimed credit for this drink.

And it's not only professional bartenders who have made this claim. One interesting story involves a wealthy Texan named Margaret Sames who claims to have created the cocktail for a party she threw at a vacation home in Acapulco in 1948. She says she combined tequila, Cointreau, and lime juice and named the new cocktail "Margarita," a Mexican version of her own name.

Unfortunately for Ms. Sames, an importer for Jose Cuervo Tequila had been running ads for a Margarita three years before Margaret held her party.

Probably the most plausible story about the creation of the Margarita is that it evolved from a nineteenth-century cocktail called the Daisy. In Jerry Thomas's 1876 book *Bar-Tender's Guide or How to Mix All Kinds of Plain and Fancy Drinks,* the Daisy combines orange liqueur, lemon juice, and one of four spirits: brandy, gin, rum, or whiskey. Suppose a bartender along the U.S.–Mexican border made a Daisy using tequila as the base spirit, and lime juice instead of lemon. If that bartender were Mexican, he or she might have referred to the drink as a Margarita—the Spanish word for *daisy.*

## Cocktail Tip:

*Use these techniques for rimming a cocktail glass with either salt or sugar.*

When rimming a cocktail glass with salt or sugar, cut a small wedge of orange, lemon, or lime (depending on the fruit used in the cocktail), and moisten the outside rim of the glass with the cut fruit. Pour salt or sugar into a saucer and slide the rim gently along the surface of the saucer until it touches the salt or sugar, which will stick to the moistened edge. Spin the glass until the salt or sugar coats the entire rim. This technique ensures that the salt or sugar coats the outside of the glass rather than the inside, where it might flavor the cocktail too much.

When salting a rim, use non-iodized salt. When sugaring a rim, use superfine or baker's sugar if you can, because finer grains stick better to moistened glass.

And consider salting or sugaring only half of the rim so your guests have the option of choosing whether to sip from the salted or sugared rim—or not. ❧

*Created over a century ago
in an elegant gentleman's
club in Burma*

# PEGU CLUB

*The Pegu Club cocktail is highly regarded by industry professionals, but not well known to the general public. In 2005, Audrey Saunders opened a bar in New York City that she named for this very cocktail. The bar became a training ground for some of the nation's leading bartenders. Unfortunately, it closed in April 2020, a casualty of the COVID-19 pandemic.*

| | |
|---|---|
| 1½ ounces | **Tanqueray Gin** |
| ¾ ounce | **Cointreau** |
| 2 teaspoons | **freshly squeezed lime juice** |
| 1 dash | **Angostura Bitters** |
| 1 dash | **Fee Brothers Orange Bitters** |

## Recipe

1. Combine all the ingredients in a cocktail shaker. Add ice cubes and shake until cold.

2. Strain into a chilled martini glass.

3. Cut a six-inch strip of lime peel with a channel knife to spray zest oil onto the surface of this cocktail.

4. Twist the strip into a corkscrew around the handle of your barspoon. Slide it off the end and drop it into the drink where it will add a little more flavor.

5. Add a Tillen Farms Merry Maraschino Cherry as an additional garnish.

## Recipe Notes

This is one of those cocktails that can easily end up being overdiluted—so shake only with larger ice cubes, and limit your shaking time to just 10 seconds, instead of the normal 12. If this abbreviated shaking time results in a cocktail that is not quite as chilled as you would like, consider placing the finished cocktail in your freezer for a few minutes.

## History

The original Pegu Club was established in Rangoon, Burma (now Myanmar), in 1871 as a social club for English gentlemen, including army officers and government officials who were engaged in an ongoing war to annex the country for the British empire. Guests could drink, dine, and stay overnight in the attractive club building constructed from teak harvested in Burma's forests in 1882.

In 1889 Rudyard Kipling paid a visit to the club and became intrigued with the stories of battles happening further north. He described his visit in his book *From Sea to Sea:*

> *There must be a few hundred men who are fairly behind the scenes of the Burma War—one of the least known and appreciated of any of our little affairs. The Pegu Club seemed to be full of men on their way up or down, and the conversation was but an echo of the murmur of conquest far away to the north.... I went out into the steamy night, my head ringing with stories of battle, murder, and sudden death.*

In 1922 the future king of England, Edward VIII, was a featured guest for dinner in the club's Great Hall.

Yet it's not the visiting dignitaries nor the attractive architecture for which the club is most remembered. Rather, it's the delicious house cocktail that was created there. As club members left Burma, they did not leave the cocktail behind. Harry Craddock, in his *Savoy Cocktail Book,* put it this way:

> *[It is] the favorite cocktail of the Pegu Club in Burma, and one that has travelled, and is asked for, 'round the world.*

The Japanese invaded Burma during World War II and converted the Pegu Club into an officers' brothel. Three years after the war ended, Burma gained its independence from Britain, and in 1962 the Burmese army took over the building as an officers' mess (a.k.a. "dining hall"). In 1965 the building was abandoned and fell into disrepair. Still, there might be a happy ending to this story. Recently the club's buildings have been refurbished and are now available for both corporate and private events.

# Cocktail Tip:

## Consider adding salt to your favorite cocktails.

My first introduction to using salt in a cocktail came from an excellent professional bartender who added salt to an Old Fashioned I'd ordered. I've since found that salt reduces the bitterness while enhancing both sweet and sour flavors in cocktails.

If you're interested in trying this technique, I don't recommend that you simply add a "pinch" of salt to a cocktail, because that's a fairly imprecise measurement. The bartender who introduced me to the concept was more precise: he made a saline solution and added a few drops to my cocktail.

You can make your own saline solution by adding 1 ounce (by weight) of non-iodized salt to 4 ounces of water. Shake to dissolve. Use a dropper to dispense the solution into your cocktails, starting with 5 drops to a standard-sized cocktail. Taste, and add more if you think it's necessary.

You can test to see whether you like salt in a specific cocktail by picking a cocktail with citrus elements, such as the Pegu Club, or one with bitter elements, such as the Boulevardier, and making two versions of it—one with salt and one without. See if you can taste a difference. If not, add a few more drops of the saline solution to the salted version. When you finally taste a difference, decide which version you prefer. But remember, the salt should always be working in the background. If the cocktail starts to taste salty, you've clearly added too much. ❧

*First appeared in Paris during World War I*

# SIDECAR

*In* The Fine Art of Mixing Drinks, *David Embury lists the Sidecar as one of the six basic cocktails that every host should learn to make. And Jeffrey Morgenthaler, in* The Bar Book, *proclaims a perfectly made Sidecar the ultimate expression of a shaken cocktail. When made with quality cognac and demerara syrup, it's a superb drink.*

| | |
|---|---|
| *1½ ounces* | *Remy Martin VSOP Cognac* |
| *1 ounce* | *Cointreau* |
| *¾ ounce* | *freshly squeezed lemon juice* |
| *¼ ounce* | *demerara syrup (see Chapter 7: Custom-Made Cocktail Syrups)* |

## Recipe

1. Combine all ingredients in a cocktail shaker. Add ice cubes and shake until cold.
2. Strain into a chilled martini glass.
3. Garnish with a wedge of lemon and a Tillen Farms Merry Maraschino Cherry.

## Recipe Notes

There are essentially two versions of the Sidecar—the French version and the English version. The French version calls for three equal parts cognac, Cointreau, and freshly squeezed lemon juice. The English version employs a higher ratio of cognac to the other two ingredients. Most cocktail writers follow some variation of the English version.

The Sidecar is often served in a glass with a sugared rim. Arguments abound around this process. I side with Jeffrey Morgenthaler, who believes you should balance the drink by adding simple syrup to the cocktail, rather than sugaring the rim of the glass, because doing so ensures the same level of sweetness throughout the cocktail. To my mind the best idea for enhancing this cocktail comes from Robert Simonson in his book *3-Ingredient Cocktails*. He recommends using demerara syrup in place of regular simple syrup. I find that demerara syrup adds depth, richness, and a pleasing mouthfeel to this cocktail that I never was able to achieve using regular simple syrup or a sugared rim.

## History

The most popular theory concerning the creation of the Sidecar goes back to World War I. Legend has it that an American Army captain riding in a motorcycle sidecar from the front lines to a bar in Paris became extremely chilled. The bartender knew cognac would be an excellent way to relieve the officer's chill, but cognac was traditionally served as an after-dinner drink. He resolved the issue by adding orange liqueur and lemon juice to a glass of cognac, creating a new cocktail for the cold captain.

Two Paris bars lay claim to being the establishment in this story: the bar at the Ritz Hotel, and Harry's New York Bar. No less an authority than the eminent cocktail writer David Embury came close to resolving the issue when he wrote:

> It was invented by a friend of mine at a bar in Paris during World War I and was named after the motorcycle sidecar in which the good captain customarily was driven to and from the little bistro where the drink was born and christened.

Embury never actually named the bistro in question, but Harry's New York Bar fits the description of "a little bistro" much better than the grand Ritz Hotel.

Even if it did not create the Sidecar, the bar at the Ritz Hotel now features a version made with 1865 Grande Fine Champagne Cognac. This cognac, which predates the great phylloxera epidemic that destroyed most of France's vineyards in the 1870s, is considered superior to any cognac produced since, which—in my opinion—makes using it in a mixed drink a cardinal sin. As the bar at the Ritz uses up the last of this fine cognac, the price of a Ritz Sidecar keeps going up. In 2017, a single cocktail cost 1,500 euros (roughly $1,650).

# CHAPTER 6

*~Clover Club~*

*~Pisco Sour~*

*~Ramos Gin Fizz~*

*~Whiskey Sour~*

*~White Lady~*

# FOAM

# FOAM COCKTAILS

*The use of foam on the surface of cocktails is well over 100 years old and can make these five cocktails great showstoppers when you have guests.*

While the foam in the Ramos Gin Fizz is partially cream-based, the foam in the remainder of these cocktails is produced entirely from egg whites. Egg whites perform other functions as well. They enhance the mouthfeel of the cocktail and smooth out particularly strong-tasting spirits. *Note:* Adding too much egg white to a cocktail can make it bland, so some restraint is in order.

Raw egg whites make some drinkers leery, but the good news is that you can make excellent cocktail foam from a carton of *pasteurized* liquid egg whites. While I get slightly thicker foam when I use fresh egg whites, one advantage of using pasteurized liquid egg whites is that they are much easier to measure. And of course, you can assure your guests that there is close to no chance of being sickened from pasteurized liquid egg whites in their cocktails.

Regardless of whether you use fresh or pasteurized liquid egg whites, I recommend that you follow these guidelines:

1.  The fresher the egg whites, the more foam they produce— so get the freshest product possible. With pasteurized liquid egg whites, I try to purchase product that has a "best by" date roughly 60 days in the future.

2.  Chilled egg whites produce less foam than egg whites at room temperature. I warm egg whites before adding them to the cocktail by pouring them into a warm (not hot) jar until they reach about 70°F.

3.  Add the egg whites to the shaker only *after* you have added all the other ingredients. Immediately shake the drink. I learned this the hard way! I once had four Clover Clubs completely assembled, including the egg whites, sitting unshaken in four glass jars on the bar. In less than five minutes, the combination of alcohol and lemon juice had curdled the egg whites. There was no *way* to resurrect the drinks. I simply threw them out.

Some cocktail writers recommend powdered egg whites, but I find that they produce a cocktail with a slightly granular consistency. I cannot recommend them.

# Three techniques for producing foam on the surface of a cocktail:

## 1. The Dry Shake

Shaking a cocktail without ice cubes is known in the industry as a "dry shake." It's the time-honored technique for generating egg-white foam. Simply combine all the ingredients, including the requisite egg whites, in a cocktail shaker, but without any ice cubes. (*Note:* If the finished cocktail calls for club soda, do not add that ingredient until you have poured the finished cocktail into its serving glass.) Vigorously shake the cocktail in the shaker for about 12 seconds.

Dry-shaking is best done over a sink. Unlike shaking with ice, shaking without ice does not create a partial vacuum during the shaking process. Thus, the ingredients can sometimes leak out of the shaker during a dry shake. If this happens, simply reset the shaker halves and continue shaking.

To maximize the level of foam, shake the cocktail shaker in a vertical motion, not horizontally as you would when you are chilling a cocktail. Finally, consider adding a wire whisk ball (see Chapter 8: *Recommended Bar Equipment*) or the spring from your Hawthorne strainer to your shaker. Either item will help emulsify the egg whites during the shaking process and will create a thicker foam.

Once you have finished the dry shake, add ice cubes to the cocktail shaker and shake again for 12 seconds to chill the cocktail. Use a Hawthorne strainer, with the gate in the "open" position, to strain the finished cocktail into your glasses. The foam in the drink will take about a minute to rise to the surface.

Most recipes for the Ramos Gin Fizz recommend using the dry shake technique.

## 2. The Reverse Dry Shake

The Reverse Dry Shake is a relatively recent technique in which you shake the drink with ice cubes to chill it, and then shake it again *without* cubes to produce the foam. Many cocktail writers believe that this is a superior technique for producing foam. I agree—and I use a wire whisk ball during the second shake to maximize foam production.

## 3. The Cream Whipper

This is the "nuclear option" of egg-white foam production. A cream whipper is normally used to produce whipped cream, but it's also quite good at producing a thick layer of egg-white foam for cocktails. For details on the cream whipper, see Chapter 8: Recommended Bar Equipment.

Here's how to proceed if you're using a cream whipper to prepare a White Lady cocktail for four people: Assemble ingredients for *five* cocktails, including the requisite egg whites, and shake each cocktail with ice in a shaker for 12 seconds. Pour four of the cocktails into four chilled cocktail glasses. Do not be concerned that these cocktails have a minimal layer of surface foam.

Pour the *fifth* chilled cocktail into the cream whipper and screw on the top. Pressurize the whipper using a nitrous oxide ($N_2O$) gas cartridge per the manufacturer's instructions. Vigorously shake the whipper for roughly 12 seconds. Dispense a half-inch layer of cocktail-flavored foam over the surface of your four finished cocktails. You may end up with extra foam, but resist the urge to add more than a half-inch of foam since doing so may make the cocktail too bland. The whole process of producing foam with a cream whipper should take roughly a minute.

*House cocktail of a
Philadelphia gentlemen's
club of the late 1800s*

# CLOVER CLUB

*Like many classic cocktails, the Clover Club was all but forgotten after its initial surge in popularity at the original Clover Club in Philadelphia's Bellevue Stratford Hotel. Luckily, it enjoyed a revival when Julie Reiner opened her highly regarded Clover Club bar in Brooklyn in 2008.*

| | |
|---|---|
| *2 ounces* | ***Tanqueray Gin*** |
| *¾ ounce* | ***freshly squeezed lemon juice*** |
| *2 teaspoons* | ***simple syrup*** *(see Chapter 7: Custom-Made Cocktail Syrups)* |
| *¼ ounce* | ***D'arbo Raspberry Syrup*** *(see recipe notes below)* |
| *1 ounce* | ***pasteurized liquid egg whites*** |

## Recipe

The reverse dry shake is the best technique for getting a nice layer of foam atop this cocktail.

1. To execute a reverse dry shake, combine the ingredients in a cocktail shaker. Add ice cubes and shake vigorously for about 12 seconds until cold.
2. Remove the ice cubes, and shake vigorously again for 12 seconds, preferably after you've added a wire whisk ball to the shaker (see Chapter 8: Recommended Bar Equipment).
3. Strain with a Hawthorne strainer (gate in open position) into a chilled martini glass.
4. Garnish with three raspberries on a cocktail pick.

## Recipe Notes

For a more thorough discussion of the various techniques for making egg-white foam for cocktails, see the introduction to this chapter.

Although a few Clover Club recipes call for grenadine (traditionally made from pomegranates), David Wondrich does an excellent job of documenting in his book *Imbibe* that most early twentieth-century recipes, including those from the Hotel Belvedere in Baltimore and the Waldorf Astoria in New York, use some form of raspberry flavoring.

To achieve the proper raspberry flavor, bartenders and cocktail writers generally recommend using fresh raspberries, or Bonne Maman Raspberry Preserves, or bottled raspberry syrup. Normally I'd assume fresh berries would make the best drink. And I admit I'm a huge fan of Bonne Maman preserves. But after trying both these options, I found that nothing beats a drink made with quality raspberry syrup.

In making Clover Clubs, I've experimented with three commercial brands of raspberry syrup: Torani, Monin, and D'arbo. Both the Torani and the Monin were disappointing, giving the cocktail a candy-like flavor. But D'arbo Raspberry Syrup makes a wonderful Clover Club and is available at fine grocery stores and on Amazon.com.

## History

This cocktail was the signature drink at the original Clover Club, a gathering of prominent attorneys, businessmen, and writers who met periodically at the Bellevue Stratford Hotel in Philadelphia starting in 1882.

The drink appeared in New York City bars—likely the result of the Bellevue Stratford's proprietor George Boldt moving to that city to manage the Waldorf Astoria hotel—where it soon became popular with the New York theater crowd. The Irish poet and playwright William Butler Yeats was said to have had his first Clover Club at a lunch gathering held in his honor at the Waldorf Astoria in 1911. Legend has it that when a tray of Clover Clubs was brought to the table, Yeats hesitantly took one. When he sipped it, his eyes lit up, and he proceeded to consume several more during the course of the meal.

## Cocktail Tip:

*Learn the story behind each cocktail,
and share it with your guests.*

One of the great ways to enhance your own appreciation of a cocktail is to learn either its history or the history of one of its ingredients. Sharing that history with your guests will make that cocktail more memorable for them as well.

For example, the Sidecar has an intriguing history dating from World War I. It involves an American Army captain riding in a motorcycle sidecar on a very cold night from the front-line trenches to a Paris bistro. The full story is in the history section of the Sidecar recipe.

Plymouth Gin, which I've recommended for several recipes in this book, is a wonderful gin with a fascinating heritage. It has been distilled in the Black Friars Distillery in Plymouth, England, since 1793, and the building that houses the distillery was built in 1431 as a monastery for the Black Friar monks. Before the *Mayflower* crossed the Atlantic to the New World, it put into harbor at Plymouth to weather a storm. According to legend, some of the Pilgrim fathers spent the night in the monastery before reboarding the ship the next morning and continuing their voyage. For this reason, the Plymouth Gin label features a picture of the *Mayflower*, and the bottle itself features an etching of a Black Friar monk. 🍸

*The national cocktail
of both Peru and Chile*

# PISCO SOUR

*The Peruvian Pisco Sour combines pisco, a South American brandy, with lime juice, egg whites, and bitters. The Chilean version uses the juice of a particularly acidic variety of lime known as* limón de pica *and leaves out both the bitters and the egg whites. The recipe below, which is based on the Peruvian version of this cocktail, makes a fine addition to your cocktail repertoire.*

| | |
|---|---|
| *2 ounces* | **Capurro Acholado Pisco** *(see recipe notes below)* |
| *¾ ounce* | **freshly squeezed lime juice** |
| *4 teaspoons* | **simple syrup** *(see Chapter 7: Custom-Made Cocktail Syrups)* |
| *1 ounce* | **pasteurized egg whites** |
| *3 drops* | **Angostura Bitters** *(see recipe notes below)* |

## Recipe

The reverse dry shake is the best technique for getting a nice layer of foam atop this cocktail.

1. To execute a reverse dry shake, combine the ingredients in a cocktail shaker. Add ice cubes and shake vigorously for about 12 seconds until cold.

2. Remove the ice cubes, and shake vigorously again for 12 seconds, preferably after you've added a wire whisk ball to the shaker (see Chapter 8: Recommended Bar Equipment).

3. Strain with a Hawthorne strainer (gate in open position) into a chilled martini glass.

4. Garnish with three drops of Angostura Bitters.

## Recipe Notes

Pisco is a brandy made from grapes. The key to making a great Pisco Sour lies in choosing a smooth, high-end pisco. My favorite pisco is Capurro Acholado, aged for 39 months. If you cannot find Capurro Acholado, Pisco Porton is a good second choice.

For a more thorough discussion of the various techniques for making foam for cocktails, see the introduction to this chapter.

## History

Although there were written recipes for Pisco cocktails as early as 1903, two men are primarily responsible for making the Pisco Sour as popular as it is today. The first was an American named Victor Morris who opened an upscale bar in Lima, the capital of Peru, in 1916. By the early 1920s, he was serving a variation on the Whiskey Sour that substituted local pisco brandy for whiskey. A few years later, one of his Peruvian bartenders, Mario Bruiget, enhanced his boss's version of the cocktail by adding egg whites and Angostura Bitters, and in doing so made the Peruvian Pisco Sour that we enjoy so much today.

## Cocktail Tip:

### When entertaining a larger group, offer one featured cocktail.

When you have several guests arriving for drinks, do yourself a huge favor: offer one featured cocktail that you've made in quantity in advance. Making several different cocktails for eight or more guests is an outstanding way to keep yourself away from the party for 15 minutes or more. Moreover, it causes some of your guests to stand around waiting for their drinks while others are halfway through theirs.

However, once I've introduced the featured cocktail, I always ask my guests individually if they'd prefer a different drink or a nonalcoholic beverage. 🐚

*Created by an iconoclastic New Orleans bartender*

# RAMOS GIN FIZZ

*The Ramos Gin Fizz is a classic cocktail from New Orleans with a history rife with memorable characters and intriguing myths. It was created by a bartender named Henry Ramos, who according to legend insisted that it be shaken for an unbelievable 12 minutes. To accomplish that 12-minute shake, Ramos hired teams of "shaker boys" who stood behind the bartenders and took turns shaking the cocktail. When one shaker boy got tired, he would pass the shaker to the next shaker boy, and so on until the requisite 12-minute period had passed.*

*The 12-minute shake is an interesting legend, but shaking for even half that time would be torturous for a home bartender working alone. In the 1930s, after Henry Ramos retired from bartending, electric blenders began to appear on the bar scene. Noted cocktail writers Charles H. Baker and Gary Regan have endorsed the use of a blender to make a Ramos Gin Fizz. After I repeatedly encountered two problems with dry shaking this cocktail (described below in the recipe notes), I now use a blender as well.*

| | |
|---|---|
| 2 ounces | *Tanqueray Gin* |
| ¾ ounce | *heavy cream* |
| 1 ounce | *pasteurized liquid egg whites* |
| ½–¾ ounce | *simple syrup (see Chapter 7: Custom-Made Cocktail Syrups)* |
| ½ ounce | *fresh lemon juice* |
| ½ ounce | *fresh lime juice* |
| ⅛ teaspoon | *Fee Brothers Orange Flower Water* |
| 1 ounce | *Schweppes Club Soda* |

## Recipe

1. Combine the gin, simple syrup, lemon and lime juices, and orange flower water in a Boston shaker. Add ice cubes and shake vigorously for 12 seconds to chill.

2. Strain this chilled mixture into a blender.

3. Place the top on the blender and turn the blender on to the highest speed setting.

4. Immediately pour the egg whites and cream through the access hole in the blender top.

5. Continue blending on the highest speed for *just* 10 seconds. (In my experiments, a 10-second blend at high speed seems to produce the maximum amount of foam.)

6. Pour the blended cocktail into a thin, chilled collins glass or champagne flute that has been filled with one ounce of club soda and several small ice cubes.

7. Gently stir once with a barspoon to blend the club soda into the drink.

## Recipe Notes

A Ramos Gin Fizz made this way should have roughly two inches of foam floating on the surface of the cocktail. Moreover, it is a dense foam, often with peaks and valleys created as the barspoon enters and exits the cocktail.

Most recipes for the Ramos Gin Fizz call for combining the above ingredients, except for the club soda, and dry shaking (without ice). I've made a great many Ramos Gin Fizzes this way—and I question the merits of using the traditional dry shake technique with this drink, for two reasons. First, dry shaking can result in disappointingly thin levels of foam on the surface of this cocktail. Secondly, I've found that dry-shaken Ramos Gin Fizzes can be prone to developing small chunks of cottage-cheese-like curds that would be an unpleasant surprise if they ended up in your guests' drinks. You can compensate for this phenomenon by double-straining the cocktail as you pour it into a glass, but that technique reduces the amount of foam in the finished drink.

Using an electric blender to construct this drink produces excellent foam and eliminates any possibility of curds ending up in a guest's glass.

Putting ice cubes in the collins glass is an idea suggested by Robert Hess in his excellent book *The Essential Bartender's Guide*. The ice chills the cocktail a little more and helps keep it chilled.

Finally, based on the reactions of my guests, I recommend ignoring the tradition of having the foam protrude an inch or more above the rim of the glass. Ideally, when you sip this drink, you want to get a little foam *and* a little liquid with each sip—a nice marriage of textures. But if a layer of foam protrudes dramatically above the rim of the glass, it means your guests' first few sips are nothing but foam, creating messy foam "mustaches" on their upper lips.

Want to try the traditional method? Here's the recipe:

Combine all the above ingredients except club soda and dry shake (without ice) for three or four minutes to emulsify both the egg whites and the heavy cream. Once the dry shaking is complete, add ice cubes and shake again for 12 seconds to chill the drink. Strain into a chilled collins glass. Pour the club soda through the layer of foam, which will cause the foam to rise above the rim of the glass. Stir gently once to incorporate the club soda, then serve.

## History

Henry Ramos supposedly created this cocktail in 1888, and it quickly became a success. For Mardi Gras in 1915, Ramos brought in no fewer than 35 shaker boys, but they could not keep up with the demand for his drink.

Ramos did not tolerate drunkenness on the part of his patrons. He believed drinking was about savoring a cocktail, and not becoming inebriated. When Prohibition took effect, he simply quit bartending, claiming he had no interest in operating an "illegal speakeasy." If all bartenders had run their bars like Ramos, Prohibition might not have occurred.

*A gentler, more refined whiskey cocktail*

# WHISKEY SOUR

*The Whiskey Sour, which has been around since the mid-1800s, is a fine alternative to whiskey neat or on the rocks. Whiskey and lemon juice are a natural combination, and the addition of egg white mellows out the harsher taste of some whiskeys and enhances what cocktail writer Kevin Liu refers to as "mouthfeel."*

| | |
|---|---|
| *2 ounces* | **Elijah Craig Bourbon** *(or Basil Hayden's for a smoother cocktail)* |
| *¾ ounce* | **lemon juice** |
| *1 ounce* | **simple syrup** *(see Chapter 7: Custom-Made Cocktail Syrups)* |
| *1 ounce* | **pasteurized liquid egg whites** |

## Recipe

The reverse dry shake is the best technique for getting a nice layer of foam atop this cocktail.

1. To execute a reverse dry shake, combine the ingredients in a cocktail shaker. Add ice cubes and shake vigorously for about 12 seconds until cold.

2. Remove the ice cubes and shake vigorously again for 12 seconds, preferably after you've added a wire whisk ball to the shaker (see Chapter 8: Recommended Bar Equipment).

3. Strain with a Hawthorne strainer (gate in open position) into a chilled martini glass.

4. Cut a five-inch strip of lemon peel with a channel knife, allowing the zest oil to spray onto the surface of this cocktail.

5. Add a Tillen Farms Merry Maraschino Cherry as a garnish.

## Recipe Notes

For a more-thorough discussion of the various techniques for making egg-white foam for cocktails, see the introduction to this chapter.

## History

Some cocktail historians attribute the Whiskey Sour to Elliott Stubb, a ship's steward who they say created it in 1872 while ashore bartending in Peru. Yet that theory holds little water since a recipe for the cocktail (without egg whites) appeared in Jerry Thomas's *Bartender's Guide,* published in 1862. It's uncertain whether Thomas himself created the drink, but his recipe *does* predate most other sour cocktails, including the Daiquiri, the Pisco Sour, the Sidecar, and the Margarita.

*A showstopper with
universal appeal*

# WHITE LADY

*In Jeffrey Morgenthaler's* The Bar Book (2014), *the author calls this elegant cocktail with its egg-white foam "absolutely sublime."*

| | |
|---|---|
| *2 ounces* | *Tanqueray Gin* |
| *¾ ounce* | *Cointreau* |
| *¾ ounce* | *freshly squeezed lemon juice* |
| *¼ ounce* | *simple syrup (see Chapter 7: Custom-Made Cocktail Syrups)* |
| *1 ounce* | *pasteurized liquid egg white* |

## Recipe

The reverse dry shake is the best technique for getting a nice layer of foam atop this cocktail.

1. To execute a reverse dry shake, combine the ingredients in a cocktail shaker.

2. Add ice cubes and shake vigorously for about 12 seconds until cold.

3. Remove the ice cubes and shake vigorously again for 12 seconds, preferably with a wire whisk ball in the shaker (see Chapter 8: Recommended Bar Equipment).

4. Strain with a Hawthorne strainer (gate in open position) into a chilled martini glass.

## Recipe Notes

For a more-thorough discussion of the various techniques for making egg-white foam for cocktails, see the introduction to this chapter.

## History

The White Lady was created by one of two bartenders, who both happened to be named Harry.

Some cocktail historians credit Harry MacElhone for creating the first White Lady in 1919 while bartending at London's Ciro's Club. His initial version combined white crème de menthe, Cointreau, and lemon juice—a curious combination of two liqueurs, and no base spirit. Roughly 10 years later at Harry's New York Bar in Paris, MacElhone modified the recipe by replacing the white crème de menthe with gin—creating what is now a classic White Lady.

Another group of historians credit one Harry Craddock for creating the White Lady while working at London's Savoy Hotel. Among this group, the White Lady is considered Craddock's most lasting legacy. Legend has it that he hid a cocktail shaker containing a White Lady inside a wall during construction of his new bar at the Dorchester Hotel in 1938. That legend was confirmed in 1979 when workers renovating the bar found a shaker containing vials of five classic cocktails. One of them was a White Lady!

Craddock's *Savoy Cocktail Book* was published in 1930. Given the fact that the recipes in it were probably compiled sometime in the mid-1920s, there is a fairly high probability that Craddock created the first gin-based White Lady several years before Harry MacElhone modified his recipe in 1929. To be clear, neither MacElhone nor Craddock used egg whites in this cocktail. That very important addition came later.

# CHAPTER 7

# CUSTOM-MADE COCKTAIL SYRUPS

*Many different kinds of cocktail syrups have been developed by bartenders over the years, but for the cocktails in this book I'm focusing on six.*

*~Basic simple syrup~*

*~Rich simple syrup~*

*~Demerara simple syrup~*

*~Vanilla demerara syrup~*

*~Mint syrup~*

*~Orgeat syrup~*

## Basic Simple Syrup

Adding simple syrup is a more-efficient way of sweetening a drink than dissolving granulated sugar in the bottom of a serving or mixing glass. This is particularly true for built cocktails constructed in a serving glass, because you're able to deliver the same level of sweetness from first sip to last. Built cocktails sweetened with sugar muddled in the bottom of the glass tend to get sweeter as the drink is consumed.

Basic simple syrup is an important staple for any bar. It consists of 1 part water and 1 part granulated white cane sugar. You will often see the following reference in drink recipes: "Simple Syrup (1:1)."

Making simple syrup yourself has several advantages. It's much cheaper than using store-bought brands. Also, it contains no added preservatives, which are often found in such brands. Those preservatives can impart an artificial taste to the syrup.

Here are two basic techniques for making simple syrup.

### The Hot Technique:

1. Add 8 ounces (by weight) of granulated white cane sugar to 8 ounces of water in a saucepan.

2. Heat while stirring until sugar dissolves.

3. Simmer the syrup on low heat for 5 minutes.

4. Allow the mixture to cool. Bottle and store in the refrigerator.

   Any simple syrup using the hot technique should last in the refrigerator for a month or more. But when strands of mold appear in the syrup, throw it out.

### The Cold Technique:

1. Add 8 ounces (by weight) of granulated white cane sugar to 8 ounces of cold water in a jar with a watertight lid. Regular granulated sugar works fine with this method, but granulated sugar labeled "superfine" or "baker's sugar" is better, as it dissolves faster.

2. Shake vigorously about 60 seconds until the sugar dissolves. (You can also use an immersion blender or a regular blender to dissolve the sugar more quickly.)

3. Use immediately or store in the refrigerator.

The "cold" technique allows you to produced syrup quickly whenever you need it. Also, a syrup made this way has slightly more viscosity, which contributes to a better "mouthfeel" for the cocktail.

However, it doesn't last quite as long in the refrigerator. But I have kept simple syrup made via the cold technique in the refrigerator for at least three weeks without any problem.

## Rich Simple Syrup

Some drink recipes call for rich simple syrup. Rich simple syrup is made with two parts sugar to one part water—2:1. To complicate matters, recipes from British cocktail books that call for *simple syrup* are generally referring to what we call *rich simple syrup,* made with 2 parts sugar to 1 part water. Rich simple syrup is best made using the hot technique described above.

## Demerara Simple Syrup

This type of simple syrup calls for demerara sugar (a coarse brown sugar similar to Sugar in the Raw) instead of granulated white cane sugar. This syrup has a richer flavor and adds a nuanced taste to cocktails, including the Old Fashioned and Sidecar.

However, demerara sugar crystals are so large that they do not dissolve easily in cold water. Consequently, the "hot" technique described above is best for making this simple syrup.

## Vanilla Demerara Syrup

To make vanilla demerara syrup, follow the recipe above for demerara simple syrup. Once you remove it from the heat, slice a 3-inch portion of a vanilla bean lengthwise. Drop both pieces into the hot syrup. Stirring occasionally, allow the two bean pieces to infuse their flavor into the syrup for 6 to 8 minutes. Remove the vanilla bean pieces and strain the syrup into a jar.

Vanilla demerara syrup in an Old Fashioned makes for a stunning upgrade to that cocktail.

## Mint Syrup

Both Mojitos and Mint Juleps are greatly enhanced by mint syrup. It's also a fine addition to simple iced teas. And it's not much more complicated to make than regular simple syrup:

1.  Combine 4 ounces, by weight, of granulated white cane sugar with 4 ounces of water in a saucepan. Heat to a simmer and stir until the sugar is completely dissolved.

2.  Add 1 cup loosely packed spearmint leaves that have been washed and separated from their stems. Lightly muddle the leaves in the syrup to release their flavor.

3.  Simmer the syrup and mint leaves for 7 minutes. (*Tip:* Simmering too long releases the mint's chlorophyll, which can make the syrup bitter.)

4.  Strain the leaves out and allow the syrup to cool. The syrup can be used immediately or stored in a jar in the refrigerator for four weeks or the freezer for months.

5.  Check out the recipes for Mint Juleps and Mojitos to see how mint syrup is incorporated in these cocktails.

In the recipe for Mint Julep, I mentioned that if you have the space to grow your own mint (even in a window garden), a variety known as Kentucky Colonel spearmint is excellent in cocktails. I think it's even better in Mojitos than the mint variety known as Mojito Mint. I have ordered live Kentucky Colonel spearmint plants from both of these sources: *thegrowers-exchange.com* and *mountainvalleygrowers.com*. I have been pleased with both suppliers.

## Orgeat Syrup

The defining ingredient in a Mai Tai is the sweet, almond-flavored syrup known as orgeat. And the secret to a world-class Mai Tai is making your own orgeat syrup.

Orgeat was first developed by the French. The clue to pronouncing it as the French do is to remember how Zsa Zsa Gabor pronounced her first name: the French pronounce *orgeat* "or-JAH," with the emphasis on the second syllable. But you'll often hear Americans pronounce the "t" at the end of the word, which has become acceptable as well, at least in this country.

1. Combine 8 ounces, by weight, of granulated sugar with 8 ounces water in a saucepan. Stir over heat until the sugar dissolves. Pour this simple syrup into a heat-resistant glass container, preferably one you can cover.

2. Process 6 ounces whole blanched almonds in a food processor for about 20 seconds until finely chopped. Add them to the simple syrup. Stir and cover.

3. Allow the mixture to marinate at room temperature for 24 hours, stirring occasionally.

4. Line a large strainer with three or four layers of cheesecloth and place it over a quart measuring cup. Pour the syrup through the cheesecloth until you are left with the moist, chopped almond pieces in the cheesecloth. Gather the top edges of the cheesecloth and squeeze the almond pieces into a ball to extract the final ounce or two of syrup.

5. Add ¼ teaspoon of Fee Brothers Orange Flower Water to the strained syrup; stir and bottle the liquid. You can store this finished syrup in the refrigerator for three or four weeks, but always shake the bottle well before using.

## Thoughts on Incorporating Gum Arabic Powder in Sugar Syrups

You may come across articles that encourage you to add gum arabic powder to your sugar syrups to achieve greater viscosity and thus enhance the "mouthfeel" of your cocktails. This technique dates back to the nineteenth century when syrup containing gum arabic powder was referred to as "gomme syrup." Gum arabic power, derived from acacia trees in Africa, is used in both food and other applications, such as painting, shoe polish, and even fireworks, so if you choose to use it in your syrups, it's important that you order the food-grade version. From my own experiments, I detect a slight increase in viscosity with such syrups, but I also get a mild aftertaste that detracts from the cocktail. Consequently, I cannot recommend it.

# CHAPTER 8

# RECOMMENDED BAR EQUIPMENT

I'VE ALWAYS BELIEVED in investing in quality tools, whether they're for working on home improvement projects or constructing cocktails. The right tool gives you a better chance of achieving positive results. And the good news is, quality bar equipment won't set you back an arm and a leg.

I hesitate to recommend a specific brand or model of bar equipment because manufacturers change products often, and a model I recommend today might not be available when you read this tomorrow. But I can say this: whenever possible, order your bar equipment from *cocktailkingdom.com*. A professional bartender in San Francisco put me onto this company years ago, and after ordering from its catalog multiple times, I have yet to be disappointed.

Here's what you need for your well-stocked bar.

## Twelve Essential Pieces of Bar Equipment

### 1. Mixing glass

For cocktails that are stirred rather than shaken, such as Manhattans and Martinis, you need a mixing glass.

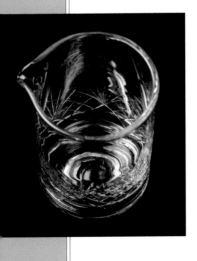

- Make sure the glass you buy is seamless. Mixing glasses with seams that join sides to bottom have a propensity to break when hot soapy water meets cold glass. As an extra precaution, I always hand wash my seamless mixing glasses in cool water.

- Choose a mixing glass with a cut crystal pattern on the outside. These patterns help you maintain your grip when the glass gets wet. Smooth-sided mixing glasses are much more likely to slip from your grasp.

- And size matters. While mixing glasses come in a variety of sizes, I recommend that you purchase a 19-ounce glass.

Both Hawthorne and Julep strainers fit perfectly on a 19-ounce glass, and this size accommodates two standard-sized cocktails perfectly.

## 2. Barspoon

For cocktails that are stirred, you need a barspoon.

- Match the size of the barspoon to the size of your mixing glass. If you choose a 19-ounce mixing glass, you'll want a 30-centimeter (approximately 12-inch) barspoon.

- In addition to using the spoon to stir your cocktails, you'll use its shaft to wrap citrus peels into corkscrew twists before placing them in your drinks. For that reason, you want a design that allows you to easily slide off those citrus twists from the top of the barspoon. Barspoons come with all manner of design elements at the top—skulls, forks, fingers—but a *teardrop* is the best design for allowing easy removal of citrus twists.

- In point of fact, the latest innovation in barspoon design is not a barspoon at all. Instead, it is a *double teardrop stirrer*. This special tool stirs more smoothly than a barspoon, which allows you to stir much faster and chill the cocktail more effectively. Try one and you'll never go back to a standard barspoon again.

## 3. An All-Metal Boston Shaker

For cocktails that are shaken, not stirred, you need a good cocktail shaker. Three kinds of shakers are on the market today:

**COBBLER SHAKER:** The cobbler shaker is usually recommended for novice bartenders. It has three parts: a metal base that holds the cocktail, a metal top with a built-in strainer, and a metal cap that covers the built-in strainer.

But cobbler shakers have two drawbacks. First, if your cocktail contains a lot of fruit pulp, the built-in strainer can get clogged before the shaker is empty. Second, the metal parts can stick together when the shaker gets cold during shaking. I bought a high-end, heavy-gauge cobbler shaker that theoretically was less likely to suffer from parts getting "frozen" together,

but I still had to use a pair of pliers to remove the cap from the shaker. As a result, I gave away that shaker.

*BOSTON SHAKER:* Like most experienced bartenders, I prefer this design for my bar. The Boston shaker allows a greater distance for the liquids to move back and forth during the shaking process, which means better chilling, aeration, and emulsification. It does require a degree of skill to use properly, but once you master that skill, I predict the Boston shaker will become your shaker of choice.

Boston shakers come in two configurations:

- A large metal section combined with a smaller, tempered-glass section
- A configuration in which both sections are metal.

All-metal Boston shakers generally produce cocktails with colder temperatures than cocktails shaken in glass-and-metal shakers. That's because thick glass absorbs some of the chilling power of the ice. The all-metal configuration has another advantage: the two parts fit together better than a glass-and-metal configuration. (The industry refers to the metal parts of a Boston shaker as "tins" even though they are usually made of stainless steel.)

*PARISIAN SHAKER:* The Parisian shaker is a cross between a cobbler shaker and a Boston shaker. Its two-piece, all-metal design resembles a cobbler shaker but without the built-in strainer.

Of all these designs, my recommendation is to go with an *all-metal* Boston shaker with a 28-ounce large tin and an 18-ounce small tin.

### 4. Hawthorne strainer

In America, shaken cocktails are typically strained using a Hawthorne strainer, while stirred cocktails are strained through a Julep strainer. In many other parts of the world, Hawthorne strainers are used to strain *both* stirred and shaken cocktails—and that could be a perfectly valid option for a home bartender. The Hawthorne strainer gives you better control than a julep strainer as you pour a cocktail into a glass.

Both Hawthorne strainers and Julep strainers feature a disc with holes or slots to strain the cocktail as it is poured from shaker or mixing glass. The Hawthorne strainer also incorporates a coiled spring along the edge of the disc. This spring helps to properly position the strainer on top of the shaker or mixing glass and provides an adjustable level of straining—from a coarse strain that allows fine shards of ice and fruit particles into the cocktail glass to a fine strain that holds them back. The adjustment is made by your index finger on a tab that opens or closes the *gate* between the edge of the disc and the rim of the shaker.

The most important quality to look for in a Hawthorne strainer is a tightly coiled spring, which results in better straining.

## 5. Julep strainer

A Julep strainer is similar to a Hawthorne strainer, but without the coiled spring.

Although you could use a Hawthorne strainer to strain both shaken and stirred cocktails, you'll look more professional (in this country, anyway!) if you use a Julep strainer to strain your stirred cocktails. Any good-quality Julep strainer from a reputable company should be a fine choice.

## 6. Cocktail jiggers

To ensure consistency from one cocktail to the next, a home bartender should always use a cocktail jigger to measure ingredients.

Qualities to look for in a jigger:

- You want a jigger that features measurement lines for ¼ ounce, ½ ounce, ¾ ounce, 1 ounce, 1½ ounces, and 2 ounces. If you can't find a jigger with all six lines, consider purchasing a second jigger with the missing measurements. Jiggers are not very expensive, and having easy and accurate access to all six measurements saves time and effort, even if it means purchasing a second jigger.

- Make sure that measurements are easy to read, either looking down from the top of the jigger or through its glass or clear plastic side. Clear OXO brand jiggers meet these requirements nicely.

- To help you avoid spills of expensive liquor, look for a jigger that doesn't require you to pour up to the rim. For example, if you're measuring two ounces of Bourbon, it's helpful to have a jigger with a 2-ounce mark that's slightly below the rim. OXO brand jiggers also meet this requirement.

## 7. Two sets of measuring spoons: regular and mini

Most home kitchens already have a regular set of measuring spoons featuring four sizes: ¼ teaspoon, ½ teaspoon, teaspoon, and tablespoon. That set will work just fine with many cocktail recipes.

However, the home bartender may want to consider a set of mini-measuring spoons to achieve even more consistency from one cocktail to the next. The mini-measuring spoon in the set I use most is the 1/8 teaspoon. For a detailed explanation, see "How much is a 'dash' of bitters?" in Chapter 9: Key Cocktail Measurements and Conversions.

## 8. Conical mesh strainer

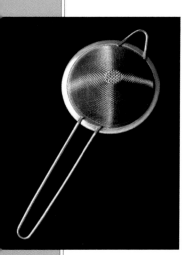

This small, fine-mesh, cone-shaped strainer has two functions. First, it's used to strain juices flowing from a citrus press into a mixing glass or shaker tin. This prevents pulp and seeds from getting into the cocktail, and it makes cleanup easier as there's less pulp to dry on the inside of the glass. Second, some bartenders like to use a conical mesh cocktail strainer to double-strain certain cocktails. They pour them in one stream first through a Hawthorne strainer and then through a conical mesh strainer positioned over the cocktail glass. This technique strains out *both* unwanted citrus pulp *and* thin shards of ice. Double-straining is particularly recommended for straining out the cream-based curds that are an occasional unwanted byproduct of a Ramos Gin Fizz.

Look for a strainer that's 3"–3½" inches in diameter. This size will fit well over mixing glasses and cocktail shakers.

## 9. Channel knife

Most people think of a channel knife as a tool to cut citrus twists for visual garnishes in their cocktails. But a good channel knife can literally make the difference between a decent cocktail and a memorable one.

Once you have cut a citrus twist over a cocktail and allowed the micro-spray of zest oil from the skin to land on the surface of the liquid, you will be amazed at how much it enhances a cocktail. A good channel knife removes a thin layer of colored peel while leaving most of the underlying white pith, which can add bitterness to the cocktail. Cut correctly, the underside of your orange twist should be mostly orange with little white pith. For how to position the channel knife under the fruit and over the cocktail to get the zest oil to spray onto the liquid, see guideline #4 in Chapter 2: Guidelines for Great Cocktails.

You'll want to look for two things when selecting a channel knife:

- Avoid "V"-shaped cutting blades. These cut too deep into the white pith. Instead, look for a channel knife with a "U"-shaped blade.

- I prefer a channel knife with a blade that points directly toward the handle, rather than one that points 90 degrees to the right or left of the handle. With these knives, it does not matter if you are right- or left-handed; you simply hold the knife stationary and twist the fruit *away* from you to cut the citrus peel off the fruit.

## 10. Hand-held citrus press

For those cocktails that contain citrus juice, squeezing it fresh is the key to making a great cocktail. Although you could use an electric juicer for this purpose, hand-held citrus presses are much more convenient for the small amount of juice needed in a cocktail.

Hand-held citrus presses have two long handles connected by a hinge. Near the hinge is a cup that holds half a piece of fruit. As the handles are brought together, a small, bowl-shaped press drops from the upper handle and presses against the fruit in the cup, causing juice to flow through the openings in the bottom of the cup. *Note:* Although it might seem counterintuitive, you want to place the fruit *cut side down* in the cup of the citrus press to avoid the juice squirting upward and into your eyes, which can be particularly nasty in the case of lemon juice.

There are two things to look for in a hand-held citrus press:

- Longer handles mean a greater mechanical advantage and more pressure applied to the fruit.

- Some hand-held citrus presses feature a gear mechanism near the hinge of the two arms that multiplies the mechanical advantage and increases the pressure applied to the fruit being squeezed.

In both cases, more pressure means more juice extracted from each piece of fruit.

## 11. Muddler

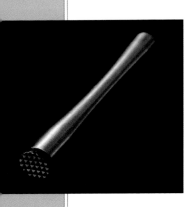

Muddlers are essential in making Mint Juleps, Mojitos, Caipirinhas, and Whiskey Smashes. Most muddlers are made from either wood or stainless steel.

- The wood version resembles a small club and is favored by many cocktail writers.
- The steel version has a nylon foot with pointed "teeth," which bruise the mint leaves or fruit to release flavor. I own a non-branded steel muddler with a plastic foot that features pointed teeth. It has worked perfectly for over a decade.

## 12. Ice bucket

If you're mixing drinks in the kitchen, you can use ice from your freezer bin as you need it. However, if you are mixing drinks in a satellite bar away from the kitchen, you'll need an ice bucket.

Four things to look for:

- You want a double-walled bucket, both to keep the ice cold and to avoid condensation on the outside of the bucket.
- You want it to be constructed of stainless steel.
- You want it to be an adequate size—about a 3-liter capacity.
- It would be great if the bucket came with a set of ice tongs or an ice scoop.

# Optional, but Helpful, Equipment for Your Bar

### 1. Half-pint cream whipper (a.k.a. whipped cream dispenser)

As mentioned in Chapter 6: Cocktails with Foam, this is the *nuclear option* of egg-white foam production. A cream whipper, which is marketed as a device to produce whipped cream, is also excellent for producing egg-white foam for cocktails.

Many brands of cream whippers, together with the nitrous oxide ($N_2O$) gas cartridges they require, are available from Amazon. The advantage of the half-pint-size whipper is that it requires fewer gas cartridges when you're making small batches of foam cocktails.

### 2. Wire whisk ball

If you like cocktails with a thick layer of foam—such as the White Lady, Clover Club, or Pisco Sour—a wire whisk ball is an incredible secret weapon. I learned about wire whisk balls when my daughter and I had Pisco Sours in an upscale Mexican restaurant. We marveled at the thickness and staying power of the foam on the surface of the drink. When I asked, the bartender shared with me his secret technique: adding a golf-ball-sized, stainless steel wire whisk ball to the liquids before shaking them in a Boston shaker. An assortment of wire whisk balls is available on Amazon, marketed for use in making protein shakes, but they work just as well for foam cocktails.

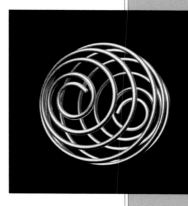

### 3. A Microplane zester

When I use a channel knife to cut orange or lemon twists, I spray the zest oil directly onto the surface of the cocktail. But channel knives can be tricky to use with limes. A better technique to get lime zest oil into a cocktail is to use a Microplane zester. You grate the zest from the skin of the lime and marinate it in lime juice. After the marination, use a conical mesh cocktail strainer to remove the zest particles before you add the oil-infused juice into the cocktail.

This technique adds a wonderful nuance to lime-based drinks, such as the Margarita and the Gimlet.

Most kitchens have a box grater, which offers four different grating surfaces. The surface with the smallest holes can be used to grate zest from the skin of a lime. However, a true Microplane zester—one that resembles a workshop file in shape and size—is more convenient and a bit easier to use for cocktail work. Some Microplane zesters even come with a plastic sleeve that slides over the zester and catches the zest as it is grated.

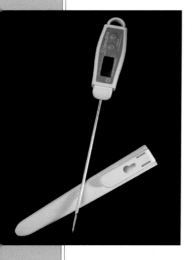

### 4. Digital pocket thermometer

Getting a cocktail to the correct temperature can greatly enhance its overall appeal. I often put finished Martinis and similar "up" cocktails in the freezer to superchill them to 19°F or slightly lower. My digital pocket thermometer gives me a quick read on the temperature of a cocktail.

### 5. Lewis bag

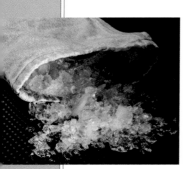

If you're a fan of Mint Juleps, you probably need a Lewis bag. Mint Juleps require crushed ice, and short of purchasing a mechanical or electrical ice crusher, a Lewis bag is the best tool for making crushed ice.

A Lewis bag is a heavy canvas bag into which you put ice cubes. Then you place the bag on a hard surface (a concrete garage floor is perfect) and beat the heck out of it with a mallet. The ice cubes quickly become crushed ice the consistency of very coarse snow—perfect for a Mint Julep and a host of other cocktails.

A Lewis bag is much cheaper than a mechanical or electrical ice crusher. And, unlike most ice crushers, it takes up almost no storage space. Lewis bags are readily available on Amazon, or you can make one from an old pair of jeans.

### 6. Ice cube tapper

If you need to crush a lot of ice cubes at one time, a Lewis bag is your best bet. But if you are simply cracking a few cubes to add to a whiskey on the rocks, an ice cube tapper is an excellent option.

I have fond memories of my father using our good silver tablespoons to crack ice cubes. Many of Mom's tablespoons were dented from Pop's ice-cracking activities. (I wish I had one of those dented tablespoons now to remember him by.)

Ice cube tappers were popular in the middle of the last century and are now making a comeback. They're a handy and inexpensive tool that you should consider adding to your bar tool collection.

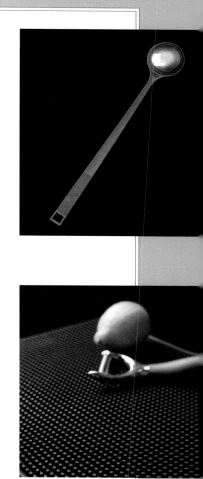

## 7. Bar mat

A bar mat is a great accessory to have. It catches spills while you're making cocktails, and it protects glasses when they get knocked over (which some will be). A tip I picked up from Lou Bustamante's *Complete Cocktail Manual* is to place my bar mat over a large plastic cutting board while making cocktails. A bar mat can collect a fair amount of liquid when you're making cocktails for a party, and when you have a plastic cutting board under your mat, cleanup is easy. You simply pick up the cutting board with the mat on top and walk it over to the sink to drain the liquid. Without the cutting board's support, the mat can sag as you move it, which means spills. Been there, done that.

Bar mats come in a range of sizes. I recommend something close to 12" x 18" dimensions.

## 8. Large square ice cube tray

For a drink such as a whiskey on the rocks or an Old Fashioned, some drinkers prefer one large ice cube in the glass rather than several smaller cubes. The large cube does a better job of keeping the drink chilled without diluting it.

Large square trays that allow you to make 2-inch cubes are readily available on Amazon. However, be careful: some trays are made of material that imparts a slight odor to the finished ice cube. Look for a tray made of food-grade rubber or silicone that's specifically designed *not* to impart odors.

# CHAPTER 9

# Key Cocktail Measurements and Conversions

**Greater precision in measuring means more consistency in your cocktails.**

Sometimes I make a cocktail and it is amazingly good. At other times, the same cocktail is merely okay. This is partly the result of mouth chemistry (what I've eaten before I took a sip) and partly a function of what I'm in the mood for. But to make sure that I eliminate as many variables as I can, I try to construct cocktails in the exact same way every time I make them. I use jiggers instead of speed pourers to measure spirits because jiggers are just about as fast and inherently more accurate than speed pourers.

But my search for consistency does not end there.

All the recipes in this book specify portions either in ounces or in measuring spoons. For the home bartender who is not under the time constraints of a professional bartender, it is generally more precise to measure a small portion of liquid, such as one-quarter of an ounce, with measuring spoons rather than jiggers. The following table converts three commonly used liquid-ounce measurements to their measuring-spoon equivalents:

*1 liquid ounce = 2 tablespoons*

*$^1/_2$ liquid ounce = 1 tablespoon*

*$^1/_4$ liquid ounce = 1 $^1/_2$ teaspoons*

On a related subject, one of my criticisms of many drink recipes is that they quote citrus juice measurements in terms of a piece of fruit, i.e., the juice of one lemon. The amount of juice you can press from one lemon can vary dramatically from one piece of fruit to another, depending on the size of the fruit and how fresh it is.

If you do come across a recipe in another cocktail book that calls for the juice of one lemon or lime, the following table will help you convert to a liquid ounce measurement:

*juice of an average-sized lemon = roughly 1 ¹/₂ ounces*

*juice of an average-sized lime = roughly 1 ounce*

Knowing these conversions allows you to determine how many lemons or limes you need to make cocktails on a given evening.

Similarly, for drinks that utilize foam from egg whites, many cocktail books simply specify one egg white. If you're using a container of pasteurized liquid egg whites, it's helpful to know:

*one large egg will provide roughly*
*1 ounce of egg white*

## How much is a "dash" of bitters?

Bartending is an industry that—in its early years—expressed measurements using quaint terms, such as a "pony"(1 ounce), a "jigger" (1.5 ounces), and a "wine glass" (4 ounces). Most modern drink recipes have dispensed with these archaic terms and simply use ounce measurements.

But one early bartending term still haunts us today: it's the term "dash," and it's used specifically in measuring bitters.

One of the great questions in the cocktail community is exactly how much a *dash* of bitters is. The actual quantity of bitters released into a cocktail will vary based on how full the bitters bottle is, the angle and velocity of the bottle as it is shaken over the cocktail, and the diameter of the opening on a given bitters bottle. Professional bartenders get pretty good at releasing the same amount of bitters each time they shake the bottle over a cocktail shaker or mixing glass. For the home bartender, it's another story. The taste of your cocktails can vary greatly, depending on the volume of the dash you put into any given cocktail.

In *The Fine Art of Mixing Cocktails* (1948), David Embury wrote that 6 dashes made up a teaspoon. After consulting with several cocktail experts, Kevin Liu claimed in his *Craft Cocktails at Home* that 6.67 dashes made up a teaspoon, not much different from Embury's estimate.

Since dashes are a relatively small measurement, if we wanted to be precise, we should probably express dashes in fractions of a teaspoon. How to do that?

The measuring spoon industry recently wrestled with this issue and standardized the conversion of the dash to $^1/_8$ teaspoon. You can buy sets of mini-measuring spoons that include one labeled "$^1/_8$ teaspoon." You may also come across sets that use the labels tad, dash, pinch and smidgen in which the one labelled dash is theoretically $^1/_8$ teaspoon. But if you get one of these sets, be sure to test that 8 spoonsful of liquid in the spoon labeled dash actually measures out to be one teaspoon in volume.

All the cocktail recipes in this book use $^1/_8$ teaspoon as the measurement for a dash. It takes no more than two seconds to measure out a dash using one of these spoons, so there is no reason for a home bartender not to use mini-measuring spoons for bitters. The benefit is much more consistency from one cocktail to the next. Amazon offers a wide selection of mini-measuring spoons.

# BIBLIOGRAPHY

America's Test Kitchen. *How to Cocktail: Recipes and Techniques for Building the Best Drinks.* Boston: America's Test Kitchen, 2019.

Arnold, Dave. *Liquid Intelligence: The Art and Science of the Perfect Cocktail.* New York: W. W. Norton & Company, Inc., 2014.

Beattie, Scott. *Artisanal Cocktails: Drinks Inspired by the Seasons from the Bar at Cyrus.* Berkeley: Ten Speed Press, 2008.

Bustamante, Lou. *The Complete Cocktail Manual: 285 Tips, Tricks & Recipes.* San Francisco: Weldon Owen Inc., 2016.

Cate, Martin, with Rebecca Cate. *Smuggler's Cove.* Berkeley: Ten Speed Press, 2016.

Charming, Cheryl. *The Cocktail Companion: A Guide to Cocktail History, Culture, Trivia and Favorite Drinks.* Coral Gables, Fla.: Mango Publishing Group, 2018.

Cheever, Susan. *Drinking in America: Our Secret History.* New York: Hachette Book Group, 2015.

Conrad, Barnaby. *The Martini: An Illustrated History of an American Classic.* San Francisco: Chronicle Books, 1995.

Craddock, Harry. *The Savoy Hotel Cocktail Book.* London: Pavilion Books, 2011.

Curtis, Wayne. *And a Bottle of Rum: The History of the New World in Ten Cocktails.* New York: MJF Books, 2006.

Day, Alex, Nick Fauchald, and David Kaplan. *Cocktail Codex: Fundamentals, Formulas, Evolutions.* New York: Ten Speed Press, 2018.

Degroff, Dale. *The Craft of the Cocktail.* New York: Clarkson Potter, 2002.

Degroff, Dale. *The Essential Cocktail: The Art of Mixing Perfect Drinks.* New York: Clarkson Potter, 2008.

Embury, David. *The Fine Art of Mixing Drinks.* New York: Mud Puddle Books, 2008.

Grimes, William. *Straight Up or On the Rocks: The Story of the American Cocktail.* New York: North Point Press, 2001.

Haigh, Ted. *Vintage Spirits and Forgotten Cocktails.* Beverly, Mass.: Quarry Books, 2009.

Harwell, Richard. *The Mint Julep.* Charlottesville: University of Virginia Press, 2005.

Hess, Robert. *The Essential Bartender's Guide: How to Create Truly Great Cocktails.* New York: Mud Puddle Books, 2008.

Hollinger, Jeff, and Rob Schwartz. *The Art of the Bar: Cocktails Inspired by the Classics*. San Francisco: Chronicle Books, 2006.

Kosmas, Jason, and Dushan Zaric. *Speakeasy*. Berkeley: Ten Speed Press, 2010.

Liu, Kevin. *Craft Cocktails at Home: Offbeat Techniques, Contemporary Crowd-Pleasers, and Classics Hacked with Science*. San Bernardino, Calif.: Self-published, 2013.

Meehan, Jim. *Meehan's Bartender Manual*. Berkeley: Ten Speed Press, 2017.

Meehan, Jim. *The PDT Cocktail Book: The Complete Bartender's Guide from the Celebrated Speakeasy*. New York: Sterling Publishing, 2011.

Morgenthaler, Jeffrey with Martha Holmberg. *The Bar Book: Elements of Cocktail Technique*. San Francisco: Chronicle Books, 2014.

Petraske, Sasha, with Georgette Moger-Petraske. *Regarding Cocktails*. New York: Phaidon, 2016.

Reddicliffe, Steve, Editor. *The Essential New York Times Book of Cocktails*. Kennebunkport, Maine: Cider Mill Press, 2015.

Regan, Gary. *The Joy of Mixology: The Consummate Guide to the Bartender's Craft*. New York: Clarkson Potter, 2003.

Regan, Gary, and Mardee Regan. *The Martini Companion: A Connoisseur's Guide*. Philadelphia: Running Press, 1997.

Regan, Gaz. *The Negroni: A Gaz Regan Notion*. Upper Slaughter, U.K.: Mixellany Limited, 2012.

Simonson, Robert. *The Old-Fashioned: The Story of the World's First Classic Cocktail with Recipes and Lore*. Berkeley: Ten Speed Press, 2014.

Simonson, Robert. *3-Ingredient Cocktails: An Opinionated Guide to the Most Enduring Drinks in the Cocktail Canon*. New York: Ten Speed Press, 2017.

Wondrich, David. *Esquire Drinks: An Opinionated & Irreverent Guide to Drinking*. New York: Hearst Communications Inc., 2002.

Wondrich, David. *Imbibe!* New York: Penguin Group, 2007.